DATE			

VICTORIAN POPULAR
MUSIC

VICTORIAN POPULAR MUSIC

Ronald Pearsall

GALE RESEARCH COMPANY
Book Tower, Detroit, Michigan 48226

CONTENTS

		Page
	List of Illustrations	7
	Introduction	11
1	The Song and Supper Rooms	16
2	The Music Hall	26
3	The Singer and the Song	40
4	Burlesque	60
5	Music in the Home	74
6	Mechanical Music	98
7	The Tonic Sol-fa Movement	111
8	The Promenade Concerts	123
9	Oratorio—Pleasure or Piety?	138
10	The Two Faces of Opera	149
11	Ballet	165
12	The Dancing Years	176
13	Outdoor Music	189
14	Country Matters	205
15	The Economics of Victorian Popular Music	219
	Appendix: Publishers' Lists of Songs and Piano Music	229
	Select Bibliography	233
	Index	237

LIST OF ILLUSTRATIONS

Evans's song and supper room (drawing by William M'Connell)   17

The Lord Raglan, Bloomsbury (courtesy The Press Association)   18

The Oxford Music Hall (courtesy The Press Association)   20

The Canterbury Music Hall (courtesy The Press Association)   23

The Grecian Theatre, alias the Eagle Saloon (from *Wonderful London*)   27

Playbill of the Britannia Theatre, Hoxton, for January 1855 (courtesy Victoria & Albert Museum)   28-29

The Oxford, on the junction of Tottenham Court Road and New Oxford Street (courtesy Victoria & Albert Museum)   31

The gallery of the Middlesex Music Hall (The Mogul) (from *The Graphic*)   32

Collins's Music Hall, Islington (from *Wonderful London*)   34

The Alhambra Theatre, Leicester Square (from *Pictorial London*)   36

1874 study of music hall backers and promoters   37

Interior and exterior of the London Pavilion (courtesy Victoria & Albert Museum)   38

'Lulu', depicted on a sheet music cover (courtesy Victoria & Albert Museum)   41

A painting by Sickert of the Old Mogul—the Middlesex Music Hall (courtesy City of Nottingham Art Gallery)   42

'Champagne Charlie'   45
George Leybourne   46
Music hall songs echoing contemporary events (courtesy
    Victoria & Albert Museum)   49
Audience queuing outside the Standard Music Hall, in the
    East End (from *Pictorial London*)   51
The Hippodrome, Nottingham   58
The Knight and Sprite, a burlesque performed at the Strand
    Theatre (from *The Illustrated Times*)   61
A tableau from the pantomime Cinderella performed at the
    Lyceum (from *The Illustrated Times*)   63
The burlesque at the Olympic Theatre (from *The Illustrated
    Times*)   65
The burlesque at the Haymarket Theatre (from *The
    Illustrated Times*)   66
An engraving by 'Phiz' of an 1856 pantomime audience (from
    The Illustrated Times)   67
The Prince of Wales' Theatre, in Tottenham Street (from
    The King)   69
A musical comedy of the closing years of the century
    (courtesy Victoria & Albert Museum)   71
Miss Kate Vaughan and Miss Nellie Farren   73
A sketch done for the magazine *London Society* in 1865   75
A cartoon of 1900 depicting Paderewski (from *The King*)   77
The unusually rapt attention of an audience of the 1880s
    (from *The Girls Own Annual*)   78
Playing the piano as an aid to flirtation   79
Soul and intensity demanded of the more lachrymose
    drawing-room ballads (from *London Society*)   81
A formal musical matinee of the mid-1880s (from *The Girls
    Own Annual*)   82
The ideal music room of the 1890s (from *The Ladies Realm*)   84
The muted tragedy of a young performer (from *The Ladies Realm*) 85
A cartoon of 1899 (from *The King*)   86
Drawing-room musicians seen through jaundiced eyes (from
    The Girls Own Annual)   89
The apotheosis of the drawing-room ballad   90

An attempt to exploit the 'Home Sweet Home' market
(from *The Graphic*)   92
The drawing-room piano as an aid to flirtation (from *Strand*)   95
A cylinder musical box (courtesy Graham Webb)   99
A John Leech cartoon in *Punch*   100
A state concert of the early 1870s (from *The Graphic*)   102
A disc musical box (courtesy Graham Webb)   103
A cartoon strip from *Cassell's Saturday Journal*, 1899   105
An orchestrion (courtesy Alain Vien, Paris)   107
The amusing history of a popular song   109
The Tonic Sol-fa singing system and the working classes in
music (from *The Graphic*)   112
The Exeter Hall (courtesy Victoria & Albert Museum)   114
The opening phrases of two popular songs with their Tonic
Sol-fa notation   116
St Martin's Hall (drawing by William M'Connell)   117
The Hanover Square Rooms (courtesy British Museum,
Crace Collection)   125
A concert at the Crystal Palace in the 1850s (from *The
Illustrated Times*)   132
Participants circling the rink to lancers, quadrilles, and
other popular dances (from *The Illustrated London News*)   134
The Queen and Prince Albert at a performance of the
oratorio St Paul at the Exeter Hall (from *The Illustrated
Times*)   136
Studies made during the 1874 Handel Festival at the Crystal
Palace (from *The Graphic*)   140
The Crystal Palace (from *Wonderful London*)   142
The interior of the Crystal Palace (from *Pictorial London*)   144
The Norwich Festival of 1866 (from *The Illustrated London
News*)   146
The Three Choirs Festival of 1866 (from *The Illustrated
London News*)   148
A production of Meyerbeer's opera *L'Etoile du Nord* at the
Royal Italian Opera House (from *The Illustrated Times*)   150
An opera audience of 1859 satirically observed (drawing by
William M'Connell)   153

Late-Victorian operatic performers as they appeared to the
    unimpressed (from *The King*)   155
Covent Garden Opera House (from *Wonderful London*)   156
The Palace Theatre (from *Pictorial London*)   158
Taglioni (from *The Ladies Realm*)   166
The ballet as 'the hot-bed of seduction' (from *The Illustrated
    Times*)   167
Fanny Elssler (from *The Illustrated Times*)   168
Grisi (from *The Ladies Realm*)   169
The pas de quatre performed by the principal ballet dancers
    of 1845 (from *The Ladies Realm*)   171
The mazurka (from *The Illustrated Times*)   179
State balls (from *The Graphic*)   180
A dancing school (courtesy Victoria & Albert Museum)   182
A dancing academy (drawing by William M'Connell)   184
An itinerant musician playing a hurdy-gurdy (from *Wonderful
    London*)   190
German band (from *London Society*)   191
A barrel-piano (courtesy Victoria & Albert Museum)   192
Working-class girls dancing in the East End streets to the
    music of a hurdy-gurdy man (from *The Graphic*)   193
A barrel-piano being played in main street in the East
    End of London (courtesy Victoria & Albert Museum)   195
Surrealist outdoor music (from *The Girls Own Annual*)   196
The bandstand in Vauxhall Gardens (from *Old & New
    London*)   197
A fair at the Licensed Victuallers' Asylum in London (from
    The Illustrated Times)   198
The A B Kettleby Brass Band in the 1890s   200
Higham's Band of 1881   202
An open-air band concert at Wimbledon (from *The Graphic*)   203
A ballad-seller (from *Pall Mall Magazine*)   210
The notorious London district of Seven Dials (from *Old &
    New London*)   213
Country dancers (courtesy Victoria & Albert Museum)   217
St James's Hall, Piccadilly (from *The Illustrated London News*)   220
The Empire Theatre, Leicester Square (from *Pictorial London*)   223

INTRODUCTION

VICTORIAN MUSIC HAD to be popular to survive. The iron laws of supply and demand operated unmercifully, and the weak went to the wall, but music forms that might at first glance seem out of place in a book on popular music were helped on their way by strange alliances.

Two such forms were ballet and opera, and, unlike today, these paid their way without any form of subsidy. The most powerful force in their perpetuation was not, as might be expected, the theatre, but the music hall. In the early days of Victoria's reign, the music halls were looked upon as instruments of mass culture, and a policy of giving the people not what they wanted but what the management thought they ought to have was pursued with diligence and courage.

It is difficult to visualise today the impact of opera and ballet on an audience whose musical experiences were restricted to street and public house music. A mysterious new dimension was opened to them. The music hall promoters were not only voicing but promulgating the most lasting Victorian theme—that if the best were offered, the public would not be content with the second-rate. This view was strongly held by many of the sages of the age, such as Ruskin. It failed in art and literature, and ultimately it failed in music.

Popular music in the long term is music that is wanted, not music that is supplied to cater for a hypothetical taste. The music hall audiences at first accepted the fare imposed upon them from above, but opera, ballet, burlesque did not reflect their life styles and did not relate to them personally.

In the same way, classical music was brought to the popular audience not through orthodox concerts, but through promenade concerts replete with gimmicks. Beethoven's symphonies were taken from the concert repertoire and re-presented to the shilling audience in isolated movements or accompanied by brass bands. When the promoters thought that the public was ready for it, an entire symphony was slily thrust into a programme. When flanked by 'monster' quadrilles and virtuoso solos for cornet-à-piston, a promenade audience would even take a work that was well ahead of its time, such as Berlioz's *Harold in Italy* for viola and orchestra.

There are a lot of paradoxes in Victorian popular music. It was the age of both the large choir and the small piano. The Victorians were both lazy and adventurous; too idle to learn to read traditional musical notation, yet they spent large sums of money and much time in learning to master the Tonic Sol-fa systems. They spent hours at dull oratorios because it made them feel pure and uplifted, yet when Wagner's music dramas were performed the middle classes flocked to them, after the upper classes had given Wagner the thumbs down after *Lohengrin* had been hissed off the stage in Paris.

The most prominent feature of the nineteenth century musical scene was that music was not departmentalised, and a man could go in one evening from a ballad concert, sniffling over 'Home, Sweet Home', to a promenade concert, revelling in a Beethoven symphony, on to a music hall, joining in the chorus of a ribald ditty, and back to a musical evening at home, where Mendelssohn's *Songs Without Words*—perhaps the most popular piano music ever published—rubbed shoulders with '*Champagne Charlie*'. There was nothing odd in taking in these various musical experiences. Queen Victoria went to see ballet when it was considered slightly disgusting, and the Prince of Wales (later

Edward VII) was able to visit the music hall with his wife without loss of prestige.

In 'high art' music it is sometimes difficult to differentiate between popular music and popular musicians. Ballet in the theatre was kept viable by the idolisation of stars such as Taglioni, and when Jenny Lind came to London the fashionable were willing to sit on the stairs of the opera house, the auditorium being packed out, the tickets changing hands at enormous prices.

The cult of the star was extensively but haphazardly practised. Theatrical agencies were early on the scene, but little was co-ordinated; the greatest coup of the theatrical agent was in spreading the legend of the Lion Comique, the music hall celebrities of the 1860s and after, though the agencies also bear the blame for the lowered standards of the music hall. Their audience sampling was rough and ready, but they, rather than management and artists, knew what the audience *really* wanted.

The amount of music written and performed in Victorian England was unbelievable. One composer alone, Charles d'Albert, had three hundred piano pieces on the market at one time (see p 231). Every week dozens of drawing-room ballads rolled from the printing presses. With the coming of the disc musical boxes, the Polyphons and Symphonions, towards the close of the century, popular songs were put on record within a few days of their first performances. The popularity of the Tonic Sol-fa movement among amateur choirs gave the music publishing industry an additional fillip, for the choral classics of the past were reprinted in Tonic Sol-fa notation.

Few could get away from music. There were barrel-organs and barrel-pianos in the streets grinding out their raucous melodies, there were German bands at every turn, and the spidery Victorian bandstands in recreation grounds and public parks are a memento to the brass band movement and the appeal of the military band. Some people were so sensitive to the constant noise of street musicians that they were forced to move house. Others were driven nearly mad by young girls practising scales on 'the altars to St Cecilia'—the piano; the coming of the cottage upright piano put this favourite Victorian instrument within the reach of all but the very poor.

It is difficult to say which was the most powerful force in the propagation of popular music—the music hall, or the piano. In 1878, there were 347 licensed music halls in London alone. No one will ever know how many pianos there were (though in Paris in 1847 there were 197 piano makers) but one music hall song sold 80,000 copies, and few people bought a song at three or four shillings a time if there was no piano to accompany it.

For most people, music in the home meant playing an instrument oneself. The phonograph and the gramophone were not parlour entertainers until the present century. Musical boxes were, until the 1870s, expensive toys with a limited repertoire. If one wanted music one played an instrument, sang, had musical friends in, or hired musicians. Few girls of the middle classes avoided being taught the piano; piano playing was replacing needlework as the occupation of the young lady of leisure.

The amount of entertainment offered in London was extensive. There were dancing saloons, assemblies (the nearest approach to modern ballroom dancing), open air dancing at the various pleasure gardens such as Vauxhall, Cremorne, and Highbury Barn, promenade concerts, both in the winter and the summer, and hundreds of theatres presenting ballet, opera, burlesque, drama, and music hall. For the more raffish, there were 'free and easies' (men only), and all kinds of sporting events—man against dog, dogs against rats, cock-fighting, and the last kickings of prize-fighting. London was short on classical concerts, chamber music, and formal piano recitals.

The provinces were less well served. Popular music was not only orientated to London, but also urban life in general. The country people did the best they could with the alien material from the big city, though the middle classes in the country and the yeoman farmers tried to emulate urban behaviour, and Pickford's were delivering the ubiquitous piano to the most remote and unlikely places. Perhaps the farmers' daughters would gain the necessary charisma.

Authentic folk song was on the decline, and the rural working classes had to make do with a bastard form, churned out by the ballad printers in the cities and sold by itinerant ballad sellers at fairs and the like. The printers of the broadsides frequently used airs in the folk repertory, giving them new words.

The quality of Victorian popular music was enormously variable. The best is perhaps contained in the comic operas of Gilbert and Sullivan; this was perhaps the best of *all* Victorian music. Music hall songs were catchy but predictable, drawing-room ballads were endlessly tedious, though several have a poignant charm. The promenade concerts made light French overtures by Auber, Hérold, and Thomas familiar to a wider audience, and these charming trifles hold a permanent place in the affection of most music lovers today. Though oratorio was extremely well attended, its appeal was mingled with a sense of duty; at its worst it was better than a sermon, at its best it was easy uplift. The 'Hallelujah Chorus' was as well known to the man in the street as 'Home, Sweet Home'.

The Victorians were certainly sentimental and aesthetically conservative, as witness the drawing-room ballad. But they were also sharp, knowing, cynical, as witness the music hall song. They also liked Beethoven's Fifth Symphony accompanied by four brass bands. But who wouldn't?

CHAPTER ONE

THE SONG AND SUPPER ROOMS

THE VICTORIAN MUSIC HALL as we know it developed from the 'saloon theatres' which existed from about 1830 to 1840, and they owed their existence to the restrictive actions of the 'patent' theatres, which had the exclusive right to put on legitimate drama. The principal patent theatres in London were the Theatres Royal in Covent Garden and Drury Lane, and the managers of these jealously guarded their rights, never hesitating to go to law when upstart playhouses tried to infringe these rights.

The theatre proper pursued its own path, cutting off the alliance with inn and tavern that had existed from Shakespearean days, and it was now the turn of inn and tavern to develop into an independent place of amusement and entertainment. Popular music in early Victorian England was associated with good food and drink, and conviviality. Weekly sing-songs and amateur group, or glee singing were supplemented in bar parlours and eating houses by the recruitment of professional entertainers, and the tavern concert was born. These were the grass roots of the music hall.

Typical of these clubs and saloons of the 1830s and 1840s were the Wrekin and Evans's. In the middle of the eighteenth century, the former came into the hands of a Mr Sims, a Shropshire man who disliked its current name and retitled it after his native hill.

Evans's, the most important song and supper rooms of its day

Sims made the Wrekin famous for Tewkesbury/ale and Shrewsbury cakes, then favoured by the young men about town. The Wrekin came into possession of a Mr Harrold, who enlarged it by knocking three houses into one. Harrold was the uncle of E. L. Blanchard, a key figure in the Bohemian raffish world of early Victorian London, and the Wrekin became the equivalent of the coffee house of Johnsonian times, the haunt of writers, actors, and musicians.

With few exceptions the clubs and saloons that formed the ancestors of the music hall were in the Covent Garden-Strand area. The Wrekin was in Broad Court, Drury Lane, a site later occupied by model lodging houses, and the visitor was encased in a world of green baize, tobacco smoke, song, gin-and-water, and the aroma of Mr Harrold's speciality, stewed cheese.

Evans's was a stone's throw from the Wrekin, off the Piazza,

Covent Garden. 'Evans's Late Joys'—Joy was a previous owner—was inscribed over a lamp that lighted the visitors down a steep stone staircase to the supper room, where one could get poached eggs on steak, devilled kidneys and red pepper, and boiled potatoes in their jackets. Restaurants at this time had not been heard of. Those who did not have access to a domestic dinner had to be content with what were described as 'à la mode beef shops and eating-houses of little pretentions'.

Evans's was frequented by Dickens, Thackeray, Douglas Jerrold, the brothers Mayhew, the journalist Sala, the humorous writer Edmund Yates, and the painter Landseer. There were no closing hours, and it was strictly a men only preserve. The original Evans was 'a bluff, fresh-coloured man, with whitish hair and had rather a bullying tone with the waiters'. He was a singer, and was noted for his rendering of 'The Englishman' and 'If I had a Thousand a Year', and he early established the tradition that

The Lord Raglan, Theobald's Road, Bloomsbury, in 1857, one of the more intimate halls

Evans's was a place for singing as well as good eating and drinking. However, under his regime the music was disorganised and casual, and it was his successor, Paddy Green, who established Evans's as a focal point of popular music.

Our conception of popular music is totally different from that of the Victorians. The early part of the evening—until midnight—was devoted to glees and madrigals sung by choir boys from Westminster Abbey, St Paul's Cathedral, and various Roman Catholic churches. Green was a Catholic, and always got part of a mass or a litany into a programme if he could manage it.

Green arranged his musical programmes with great care, and traditional songs such as 'The Hardy Norseman', 'Oh! Who will o'er the Downs so Free?', 'Down in a Flowery Vale', 'The Silver Swan', 'The Chough and Crow' and 'All Among the Barley' were permutated so that the audience would not get bored with them.

At midnight the boys went home, and a variety of singers took their place, such as Charles Sloman, 'the only English *improvisatore*' who sang doggerel verses alluding to the dress or manner of any member of the audience who took his fancy:

And now I see a gentleman who's got a silken wipe;
He's smokin' a cigar now, he'd sooner have a pipe.
And there is his companion, who all the ladies love;
He's putting down his hat now, and taking off his glove.

Sloman was one of the first of the traditional music hall singers. It was said that he had not a musical note in his head; his voice, always husky, sounded as though he was suffering from bronchitis. Style and deportment carried him through. He worked a large number of halls and saloons, including the White Conduit House, the Union Saloon, Shoreditch, the Eagle Tavern in Mile End, the Temple of Harmony in Whitechapel, the Cider Cellars and the Coal Hole, and Vauxhall Gardens.

His repertoire included both serious and comic songs, and he also composed songs for fellow singers at Evans's, such as Henry Sidney, a dismal dirge-like singer very popular on Boat Race nights, who specialised in uplift songs such as 'A Quiet Sort of Man', 'Let the World Jog Along' and 'A Rolling Stone Was

The Oxford Music Hall in 1861, *depicting the close alliance between entertainment, food and drink*

Never Known to Gain Much Moss', varying his programme by 'discussing certain debatable topics in a quiet sort of way'. The association of uplift songs with smutty 'spoken business' was later brought to a fine pitch by the great music hall stars of the 1860s and after.

Henry Sidney later became chairman at Collins's Music Hall, Islington, and died in 1870. Sloman died a pauper in the Strand Workhouse in the same year. His speciality song was called 'The Wolf' ('Locks, bars and bolts are rent asunder . . . now the wolf he nightly prowls!') and when he was too old to sing at Evans's he was made chairman at the Middlesex Music Hall, known as the Mogul, in Drury Lane, where he was repeatedly requested to do 'The Wolf'.

Another of Evans's singers was Sam Cowell, who specialised in Cockney songs and parodies, often combining the two as in his parody of Hamlet:

A hero's life I'll sing, his story shall my pen mark;
He was not the King, but 'Amlet, Prince of Denmark.
His mammy, she was young, the crown she'd set her eyes on;
Her husband stopped her tongue; she stopped his ears with
    pison.

Two of his songs, 'The Rat-catcher's Daughter' and 'Villikins and his Dinah', ill-starred lovers who 'vos a-buried in von grave' were kept in the music hall repertory well into the closing quarter of the century. Evans's was a starting point for Cowell. He was paid seven and sixpence a night plus two hot drinks, and realising that he could make more elsewhere, he began to take liberties with the audience and with Paddy Green, his ad libbing sailing closer to the wind and his time-keeping becoming erratic. 'Mr Cowell is late again', Paddy Green cried, 'You've made him your god, gentlemen, but, by God! he shan't be mine!' and when Cowell arrived Green sacked him, whereupon Cowell went to one of the new-fangled music halls, where he commanded eighty pounds a week. In the early 1860s he went to America, but returned to England in 1864 and died soon afterwards.

J. W. Sharpe was another singer at Evans's. Born in 1818,

Sharpe died in 1856 in a Dover workhouse. He projected the image of a London swell, and his songs included 'Who'll buy my images?', 'Pity the downfall of poor Punch and Judy', 'A dainty plant is the cabbage green', 'Lively Flea', and 'There's a good time coming'.

The life of the song-and-supper singers was hazardous. The best of them managed the step from saloon to music hall, but for the rest, as soon as their audience tired of them it was either the workhouse or being a chairman at a music hall, another post that depended on the goodwill of the audience. In a sense, they were the old outdoor ballad singers in an indoor situation, and did not hesitate to hawk their songs from table to table for between half a crown and five shillings.

The words of their songs were obtained from a wide variety of sources. Sometimes they were written by the singers themselves, sometimes by habitués, such as E. L. Blanchard who wrote the words to a song burlesquing the 1851 Great Exhibition, 'Nobody in London'. Cowell's 'The Rat-catcher's Daughter' had an odd author indeed, the Reverend Edward Bradley who under the pseudonym of Cuthbert Bede wrote the best-selling *Adventures of Verdant Green* (1853-57).

W. C. Evans had handed over the proprietorship of Evans's to Paddy Green in 1844. Green died in 1874, having outlived Evans's. Green had always preserved a certain decorum at Evans's, and this had both prevented it from developing and prolonged its life, for men such as Thackeray preserved an affection for it and patronised it even when it had been superceded by new enterprises. The best of the singers used it as a stepping stone, and its entertainers were seen, in retrospect, to be pathetic rather than amusing—such as Herr van Joel, a tall Dutchman with a smooth face who sold cigars from table to table and also ascended the platform every night and yodelled and gave an imitation of farmyard animals with the aid of a little amateurish ventriloquy and a walking stick.

Eventually women were allowed into these once men only precincts, and were permitted to watch the proceedings through a grille. Obeissance was being made to the spirit of the age, but

The Canterbury Music Hall in 1856, the first of the great music halls

to no avail. Evans's had not moved with the times, and although it survived longer than most song-and-supper rooms of its vintage, it could not compete with its brash progeny, the music hall.

However, it did out-live its contemporaries, the lively and exciting Coal Hole and Cider Cellars, where almost anything went, where songs of extreme obscenity and blasphemy were rendered to an audience that found Evans's slightly *passé*. At these, relates Serjeant Ballantine, lawyer and man about town, 'there were some good songs excellently sung, but there were others of a degrading and filthy character. It seems strange that in places undoubtedly frequented by gentlemen, obscenities of this description should have been encouraged; but it must be remembered that in those days there were many coarse features throughout society'.

Places such as the Coal Hole and Cider Cellars were a safety valve to counter the effects of a repression that were to make the prurient middle classes the dominant force in Victorian life. In these underground saloons the audience could escape from their public straight-jacket, and could join in the choruses of the ribald songs and respond whole-heartedly to the pointed innuendo.

The event that made the Coal Hole and the Cider Cellars a must was the singing by W. G. Ross of 'Sam Hall', the story of a chimney sweep going to be hanged. 'He had begrimed his muzzle to look unshaven', related Percival Leigh, a writer for *Punch*, 'and in rusty black clothes, with a battered old hat on his crown, and a short pipe in his mouth, did sit upon the platform leaning over the back of a chair, so making believe that he was on his way to Tyburn'.

The words, sardonic and macabre, each verse ending with the phrase 'Damn them all', the last verse ending with 'Damn you all' (the damn sometimes replaced by another four letter word that shall be nameless), were set to a dismal psalm tune, and replete with curses and oaths. Thackeray had been deeply impressed by Ross and 'Sam Hall', and repulsive and nightmarish as the song was, he considered that the way it was acted and sung constituted 'a great moral lesson'.

F. C. Burnand related in his autobiography how he, a schoolboy at Eton, went to see Ross do 'Sam Hall'. The Cider Cellars were in Maiden Lane. Burnand and his cousin penetrated the depths of this fascinating and forbidden place, into the inner sanctum where Ross was to give his famous impersonation of the man going to the gallows. Burnand's awe did not stop him going back to Eton and giving an impression of Ross, the profanity of the expressions, that prevented Serjeant Ballantine from quoting the verses, not proving a barrier to juvenile fun.

Ross, before his success, had been a minor actor. He had been barred from Evans's, where a degree of decorum had always reigned, but when the stranglehold of Victorian puritanism had finished the Cider Cellars—the building became a 'School of Arms and of Athletic Exercises' in 1864—he became a super at the Gaiety Theatre.

The Coal Hole also featured Ross. The Coal Hole was situated in Fountain Court, Strand, and had been acquired by William Rhodes in the 1820s. Although women were not admitted into the audience, there were women singers, an exciting new innovation. Another entertainment that the Coal Hole had in common with the Cider Cellars was the 'Judge and Jury', organised by 'Baron' Renton Nicholson. In 1837 Nicholson had started the satirical paper *The Town*, specialising in libel, and in 1841 at the Garrick's Head Hotel, Bow Street, he initiated this new kind of amusement in which Nicholson, in correct judicial attire, presided as judge over mock trials, mainly dealing with sexual offences, in which *double-entendre* ran riot. The audience acted as jury.

This show moved in 1851 to the Coal Hole, affronting respectable opinion, and then to the Cidar Cellars. Although 'Judge and Jury' brought in a new audience, it ultimately killed these establishments, as the singers had to key up their offerings to be in line with the accompanying entertainment. The old regulars, who could take 'Sam Hall' and the gusty saucy song, were embarrassed by the extreme licence of 'Judge and Jury', and took their custom to the growing music hall. Finally, 'Judge and Jury' moved to a house in Leicester Square, combined with *tableaux vivants* and *poses plastiques* (Victorian striptease), but the aura of flagrant indecency hung around the Coal Hole and the Cider Cellars and they soon closed. The Coal Hole was rebuilt, and renamed the Occidental Tavern.

CHAPTER TWO

THE MUSIC HALL

THE AUDIENCES AT Evans's, The Coal Hole, and the Cider Cellars, were in-groups, belonging to a sharp and knowing class which was not apologetic about listening to glees and madrigals sung by choir boys, and could go from these without loss of face to bawdy songs after midnight had struck. They did not go to the song and supper rooms specifically for the music, but for the food, the drink, and the atmosphere. The song and supper rooms were, in effect, very informal and unstuffy men's clubs.

When the coming of railways made the population more mobile, when it was possible to visit London on cheap excursions, then this audience changed. Handbooks were published listing where a good time was to be had, and country bucks poured eagerly into these once exclusive places, their ideas of entertainment grosser than those of the original patrons of the song and supper rooms.

Things were changing, too, in the inner suburbs. London was increasing in size at an alarming pace, and the population demanded entertainment and amusement. They were too far from the traditional pleasure centres of the Strand and the surrounding streets; they wished for something nearer home. In 1834 there had been tea gardens known as the Shepherd and Shepherdess just off what was then known as the New Road (now City Road).

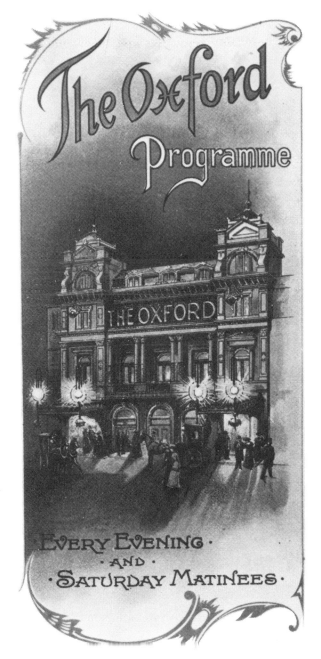

Perhaps the most celebrated of all the music halls, the Oxford, on the junction of Tottenham Court Road and New Oxford Street. Most of the famous artists of the time passed through the Oxford

The gallery of the Middlesex Music Hall (The Mogul) in 1872. It is interesting to compare this engraving with the painting by Sickert of the same subject

and a policy was formulated giving the mass audience not what they wanted but what it was thought they ought to have. *Punch*, no respecter of innovation, was impressed by the artistic aims of the Canterbury, referring to the picture gallery annexe as the 'Royal Academy over the water'.

But Morton was to establish the Canterbury as a musical centre that owed nothing to the bawdy of the song and supper rooms or the sing-songs of the theatre taverns. By some quirk, Gounod's opera *Faust* fell into the public domain through defective international registration. Morton could not present this with scenery, costumes and action, for this would have been infringing the Stage Play Act which unfairly protected the West End theatres, giving them sole rights of production. So Morton presented what he described as an operatic selection, the singers standing in rows as in an oratorio or a choral concert, accompanied by an excellent orchestra.

These performances of *Faust* ran for a considerable time, and by the time the managers of Her Majesty's Theatre in the Haymarket and the Covent Garden Theatre took note of it, the tunes from *Faust* were being whistled in the streets by the errand boys.

The success of the Surrey Music Hall and the Canterbury led other owners of saloons and taverns to convert their properties into music halls. The Mogul Saloon in Drury Lane was renamed the Middlesex Music Hall in 1851, the Seven Tankards and Punch Bowl in Holborn became Weston's Music Hall in 1857, and between the years 1851 and 1864 a large number of saloons changed their names and their status. There were also many custom-built music halls.

Wilton's of Whitechapel dated from 1856, the South London Palace, 1860, the Bedford, Camden Town, 1861, Deacon's of Clerkenwell, 1861, Collins's of Islington, 1862, the Royal Standard Music Hall, 1863, the Metropolitan Music Hall, 1864. The 1860s and 1870s were the golden decades, and with the increase in size, some of the informality went. In 1860 the Alhambra, in Leicester Square, a magnificent Moorish structure originally called the Panopticon designed 'for every startling novelty which science and the fine arts can produce', was

Collins's Music Hall, Islington, the last of the London music halls to close. This photograph was taken in the 1920s

converted to have a stage and a proscenium. The simple platform was abolished, and the role of the chairman became less important.

In 1869 the South London Palace was likewise converted, followed by the Oxford Music Hall in 1873. Like the Canterbury, the proprietor of the Alhambra did not equate popular entertainment with low standards, and in 1865 produced an ambitious ballet, from Auber's opera *L'Enfant Prodigue*. As in the case of the condensed version of *The Tempest* that Morton put on at the Canterbury, legal proceedings were started under the Stage Play Act (6 & 7 Vict. c. 68). The result of the action was unsatisfactory, depending on a quibble as to whether this ballet was a distinct story with a coherent intelligible action or a *divertissement*, but Frederick Strange, the owner of the Alhambra, felt that he had won a victory, and almost immediately put on a pantomime scene called *Where's the Police?* in which there was clearly a story line. The magistrate at Marlborough Street Court inflicted the maximum penalty—£20 a performance for twelve performances and costs.

It was clear that the music hall was being hamstrung by archaic and unfair rules, and in 1866 the music halls and variety theatres managed to get a House of Commons select committee to inquire into the position, to at least find out what constituted a stage play. They were encouraged by what was happening in France, where Napoleon III had fixed the status of music halls, permitting them to put on operettas, ballets, vaudevilles, pantomimes and light pieces.

Fortunately the chairman of the committee was George Goschen, Liberal MP for the City of London, Chancellor of the Duchy of Lancaster, and he was in favour of greater freedom being extended to the music hall. The way was set clear for the seemingly endless prosperity of the music hall. However, the Alhambra, which had encouraged court action by openly flouting the Stage Play Act, was not to share in the spoils. Frederick Strange overstepped the mark once more by producing in 1870 a ballet called *Les Nations*, at which the cancan was performed.

This ballet ran for five weeks, but the end of the run coincided with the renewal of the Alhambra s licence. The establishment

The Alhambra Theatre, Leicester Square, opened in 1854 as the Panopticon on the lines of a Polytechnic. It closed down, reopening in 1858 as a circus. This too failed, but when it was turned into a music hall is succeeded magnificently; the home of music hall ballet, the Alhambra had an orchestra second only to that of the Royal Opera House, Covent Garden

considered that the Alhambra had been a thorn in its side for too long, and without warning and with little discussion the licence was withheld.

The success of the music halls that put on programmes of ballet and opera demonstrate to us that the Victorian definition of popular music was wide. All music was popular music. Nevertheless, as the years went by it was clear that some music was more popular than others, and music halls that catered for the tastes of their audiences rather than tried to improve them with 'art music' were seen to be doing rather better than the others.

Spectacular ballets, grand stage trickery, glorious panoramas, these did not vie in appeal with the celebrity singer, and after the years of adventure the music halls were reverting to their initial role. A new generation of singers was needed to replace the song-and-supper room men. Sam Cowell, the doyen of Evans's, was not too old to adapt, and went to the Canterbury, but most of the others lacked the charisma that the music hall demanded.

The impression given by modern revivals of music hall is that the bulk of the programmes were made up of novelty turns—illusionists, knock-about comedians, gymnasts, ventriloquists, and the like. This was not true. Song made up the largest part of the entertainment, the centre-piece of which was the performance of the celebrity singer. These singers, relentlessly promoted, provided by the managements with a carriage and four, were paid enormous salaries. They frequently performed in several music halls a night, so great was the demand for their services, and their speciality songs. One of these singers—the Lions Comique as they were collectively called—was the 'Great' MacDermott. His daily programme in 1878 was:

4.15	8.15	Royal Aquarium
	9.10	Metropolitan
	10.00	London Pavilion
	10.50	Collins's

The backers and promoters of Victorian music hall kept very much in the background, but this revealing 1874 study has an air of truth about it

The interior and exterior of the London Pavilion, built after Piccadilly
Circus had been enlarged in 1885-86 to make way for the new road,
Shaftesbury Avenue

The smaller halls were unable to pay the salaries these men demanded, and had to be content with the smaller fry who tried to emulate the Lions Comique. Their troubles were only just beginning. In 1878 a law was passed demanding a 'certificate of suitability' for music halls and variety theatres, entailing a proscenium wall dividing the stage from the auditorium and the provision of a safety curtain. The less affluent theatres could not afford to pay for such alterations.

A further blow was dealt by this law. Liquor was banned from the body of the hall. Thus the link between food, drink, and entertainment that had existed in popular entertainment was broken. The richer theatres faced this by having a promenade at the back of the stalls, so as not to risk losing the 'wet money', but the poorer halls could not cope with the new demands. Over the country, two hundred music halls closed; these included such well-known halls as Wilton's and the Winchester (formerly the Surrey Music Hall, the first music hall, a pioneer in the presentation of nigger minstrels and black-faced shows).

A rationalisation of the whole music hall industry set in, and syndicates were formed, the chains of Empires, Palaces, and Hippodromes throughout the country being the legacy of the syndicates. Big business killed the intimacy of the old music hall, just as the music hall had killed the saloon.

One of the features of music hall was the chairman. He acted as liaison between the performer and the audience, and would also serve as a straight man to favoured artists. He introduced the acts, and it was considered a privilege to be invited to sit at his table, analogous to being asked to sit at the captain's table on board ship. He had to be quick-witted and resourceful, ad libbing when things on stage were going demonstrably wrong, and it is not surprising that many chairmen had been music hall performers.

With the new look in the music hall the chairman was abolished, tip-up seats were installed, ventilation, lighting, and comfort improved, and opulent schemes of decor were carried through, resulting in a colourful vulgarity that was only paralleled by the cinema-building mania of the 1920s and 1930s.

CHAPTER THREE

THE SINGER AND THE SONG

THE MUSIC HALL song does not fit into a neat category. The best songs were catchy and memorable, but these existed alongside tepid ditties that died almost as soon as they were born. There was a certain area where the music hall owners were unsure of their ground, and the success of the prestige halls in promoting music that would not have been out of place in the opera house or the concert hall encouraged some managers to put over songs which were neither one thing or the other, a hybrid between the drawing-room ballad and the true music hall song.

As the music hall developed from its small beginnings, so did the audience change. The song and supper rooms had a clientele that was middle class with upper class slummers, while the music halls catered for the whole social spectrum, the make-up of the audience varying with the site and size of the hall. The most startling change however was the increase in the proportion of women in the audience, though the songs that were aimed at them were small in number.

The three major classes into which the music hall songs were divided were (a) comments on contemporary life and events (b) love and domestic songs (c) uplift and patriotic songs. The repertoire included a great deal of Cockney material, for although the audience was a cross section, and could include the

The music hall could be gay and raffish, or pedestrian and dull. Although Lulu's costume was daring for the time, this does not seem to have offended the Prince and Princess of Wales when they visited the music hall in 1871

Prince of Wales (later Edward VII), a frequent visitor to the music hall, the ordinary Londoner provided the basic support.

There may, of course, be some argument as to whether there is such a thing as the ordinary Londoner. The lower middle classes, the clerks and shopkeepers with their wives, the improved working classes, these were sharply individual, only sharing a cynicism, a sentimentality lying close to the surface, and an aversion to authority. The aim of the music hall star was to weld this audience into one, using the medium of the song.

Such an audience was not involved in the spectacular coups of the Canterbury and the Oxford. The ballets and the grand music were apart from them. They watched but did not participate. The celebrities altered this, working upon their audience with an instinctive skill, urging the blank faces in the stalls and the

A painting by Sickert of the Old Mogul (the Middlesex Music Hall)

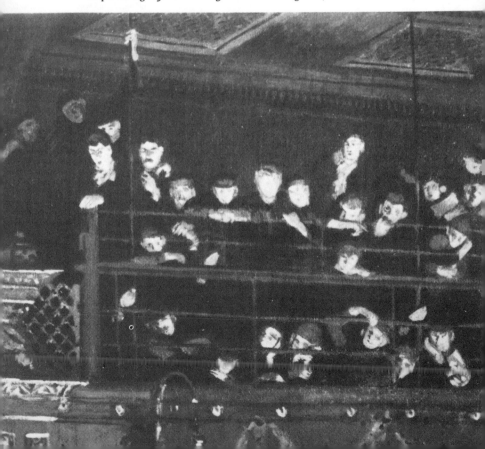

gallery to join in. They did this in a number of ways, by identifying with them and pandering to their prejudices and whims, or by mock-alienation, by jeering at them and patronising them.

The latter was a hazardous path, but so great was the assurance of the best of the Lions Comique, so idolised were they, that they could accomplish this with an ease that in retrospect is amazing. The great age of the music hall was the age of the swell. The fashionably or stylishly dressed person for whom the appellation had been coined in 1811 was not quite the swell of the 1860s and 1870s. The mid-Victorian swell strutted and postured, his self-importance hiding a hint of social unease.

The music hall audience had a love/hate relationship with the swell, both envying him and disliking him. It was a stroke of genius for the Lion Comique to adapt the persona of the swell, for he could both patronise and taunt, yet assure the groundlings that he was one of them, joining them in contempt for new trends and movements such as the aesthetic movement of Whistler and Oscar Wilde. Of course, he was not. The Lions Comique were professionals who had graduated to their eminence via hard work.

Four of these men stand out from the rest. Arthur Lloyd, the first of them, is the least characteristic, going more for the line of the 'little man'. Lloyd's father was a Scots comedian, and Lloyd was trained as an actor, moving from Glasgow to London in 1862 or 1863. He wrote the words and music for many of his songs, and also wrote a four act drama produced in Newcastle-on-Tyne in 1887. In social life Lloyd was a quiet and taciturn man with a passion for mismanaging theatres. He had a vast repertoire, including upwards of two hundred songs of his own composition including the incredible best-selling 'Not for Joseph' (80,000 copies of the sheet music sold). He was very strong on nonsense songs with titles like 'Chillingo-Wullabadorie' and this verse from a 'Japanese' nonsense song is characteristic of this genre:

> Pollywollyamo, nogi, soki,
> Pollywo-a-lumpa shoes two tees,
> Slopey in the eye; flat-nosed beauty,
> Pollywollywolly! Jolly Japanese.'

George Leybourne, real name Joe Saunders, was an engine-fitter in the Midlands up to London for a holiday. He had tried his hand in 'free and easies' (inns where amateur singing was encouraged), and hearing Lloyd sing he determined to be a comic singer. He made his debut at the Canterbury about 1868 and was soon earning a hundred and twenty pounds a week. Taking the lead from his rival the 'Great' Vance, he adopted the style and posture of the swell, and lived up to it, dying in poor circumstances at the age of forty-two. Tall, handsome, elegant, dressed in the fur coat that was obligatory for music hall stars, Leybourne magnetised his audience. The impresario George Edwardes declared after Leybourne's death that he would pay £1,000 a week to another such as he.

Alfred Vance was a lawyer's clerk in Lincoln's Inn Fields before turning to acting on a provincial circuit. Born in 1840, real name Alfred Peck Stevens, Vance had had a fairly wide stage career before reaching the Metropolitan, Edgware Road, about 1864, playing Shakespeare in Manchester, and doing one-man shows playing twenty different parts. He had also been a clown in a pantomime at the St James's Theatre. Marginally first with the role of the music hall swell, Vance carried this image into his private life too.

There is an interesting vignette given by the actor Charles Brookfield. Vance travelled from theatre to theatre in the course of a single evening giving his performance, calling in at various pubs on the route. Brookfield met him in a pub next to the Haymarket Theatre. After a few minutes' conversation Brookfield said that he must be off. Vance asked him where he was going. 'Only next door', replied the actor, 'to the Haymarket Theatre'. 'Well', exclaimed Vance cordially, 'take my carriage; it's doing nothing'. This was style, and the Victorians loved it.

Vance outlived Leybourne, but hardly outlasted him. The changing form of music hall, intimacy and rapport with the audience being sacrificed to larger theatres and profits, left him stranded, and he died working the Sun, Knightsbridge, deserted by the fickle public.

The last of this quartet, G. H. Macdermott, had a commanding

CHAMPAGNE CHARLIE

THE GREAT COMIC SONG WRITTEN & SUNG BY
GEORGE LEYBOURNE.
Music by Alfred Lee.

'Champagne Charlie' was one of the great popular songs of the mid-Victorian period, sung by George Leybourne. An example of Victorian advertising, the song was subsidised by the champagne shippers to the tune of £20 a week in free fizz

It is unusual to see George Leybourne out of costume; Leybourne was one of the stars who projected his music hall persona into his personal life. He was a swell off the stage as well as on it.

presence with a gift of precise articulation. He was the great master of the double entendre. Although he came later to the music hall stage than either Vance or Leybourne—debut London Pavilion about 1873—he had done his apprenticeship at the Grecian Saloon, City Road, as an actor. Macdermott was the archetypal working man who made good; born Farrell, he was a bricklayer's labourer before entering the Navy, where he tried his hand at amateur theatricals.

Like Leybourne, Macdermott arrived on the music hall scene by accident. A playwright named Arthur Pettitt had written a song with the refrain 'If ever there was a damned scamp', and to fill up a holiday Macdermott procured an engagement at the London Pavilion. 'The Scamp' proved a great hit, and Macdermott never looked back, for unlike Lloyd who lost his money managing theatres, Macdermott, when he was barred from the West End on account of the extreme indelicacy of his ad-libbing and spoken business, bought a string of music halls in the East End and prospered until his death in 1901.

These were the successors to Sloman, Sharpe, and Henry Russell, but there is a difference. The Lions Comique were not ballad singers come in out of the cold, but all round entertainers, the spoken business between the verses often as well rehearsed as the apparent ad-libbing of television comedians. Style, deportment and delivery were as important as the material. It is therefore difficult to judge the effect of the songs they sang from the music and the text, as difficult as future historians will find when determining why 'The White Cliffs of Dover' was so poignant when sung in the 1940s by Vera Lynn. The songs did not exist in a vacuum; they were an integral part of the environment of the music hall, along with food and drink in the auditorium, and the sense of well-being that comes from several hundred people sharing the same enthusiasm in a closed space.

This categorical commitment to unadulterated pleasure was resented by those who could not or would not participate. Sir Hubert Parry's diatribe against the music hall song in 1899 tells us more about Parry's prejudices than about the song:

> The modern popular song reminds one of the outer circumference of our terribly overgrown towns . . . It is for the people who live in those unhealthy regions, people who have the most false ideals, who are always scrambling for subsistence, who think that the commonest rowdyism is the highest expression of human emotion; for them, this popular music is made, and it is made, with a commercial object, of snippets of slang.

There were others who saw the music hall song as a phenomenon that could be adapted to laudable pursuits. In 1878, following the wide success of Leybourne's song, 'Champagne Charlie', William Booth, forming the dissident Evangelical sects into the Salvation Army, used the tune of that music hall song as an aid to moral rehabilitation. The Evangelists Dwight L. R. Moody and Ira D. Sankey also observed the wide currency and powerful appeal of popular song, and when they joined forces in 1870, issuing their *Sacred Songs and Solos*, the lessons of music hall and popular song were evidently learned. Memorability and even a religious catchiness were more important than academic merit. Moody and Sankey visited Britain in 1873 and 1883, and repaid their debt to popular song, for the music hall immediately used their hymn tunes, with words that were either amusing or blasphemous, depending on viewpoint.

One can get an idea of the range of the music hall audience's interests by a study of the song titles, and it is immediately apparent that this audience was well aware of the trends of the time. When worked on by the celebrity singers it could be intensely loyal and patriotic, and the tears which it was collectively encouraged to shed for personalities such as Gladstone (when he died) were by no means synthetic. During the time of the Russo-Turkish War (1877-79), Macdermott's song 'We Don't Want to Fight But By Jingo If We Do' not only gave a new word to the English language, but almost precipitated England into the war by arousing popular feeling on behalf of the Turks, misleadingly identified as the poor little fellows confronted by the Russian bear. It was believed that Macdermott was in the pay of the Conservative Party, which was interested in meddling in that war.

The music hall audience was acutely aware of contemporary events. There was a vast fund of feeling for the underdog, and a clever singer could tap this at will. It was a self-evident fact that Britain was the greatest country the world had ever known or

(*Opposite*) *Music hall songs echoed contemporary events, and the Bloomer Movement, 'the rational dress', introduced into America in 1849 and into Britain in 1851, provided perfect material. The 'Bloomer Polka' was a multi-purpose work, suitable for music hall, drawing-room, or burlesque*

THE BLOOMER POLKA

COMPOSED & INSCRIBED TO

Mrs COLONEL BLOOMER

BY

J. J. BLOCKLEY.

AUTHOR OF THE OBERON POLKA

DUFF & HODGSON'S OXFORD St

Pr 2/

ever would know, greatest in stature and greatest in righteousness, having therefore *carte blanche* to meddle in the affairs of other nations that were less fortunate. It is not to be wondered at that common people of the age were at one with Palmerston, who felt much the same way.

Julius Haynau was an Austrian general, who in the campaigns against Italy (1848-49) gained notoriety by his flogging of women when he captured.Brescia. Appointed dictator of Hungary after he had subdued it, he came to England in 1850, where he was assaulted and severely handled by draymen of the famous Barclay and Perkins' brewery. This was nearer at home than the dim misunderstood trouble between Russia and Turkey three decades later, and dearer to the hearts of all freedom-loving music hall audiences. 'General Haynau and the Draymen' was an instant success.

At that time Hungary was a happy quarry of music hall material. In 1848 Louis Kossuth, inspired by the French Revolution of that year, had demanded an independent government for Hungary in place of the corrupt Hapsburg dynasty. To a certain extent he got it, before Haynau subjugated the country. The 'Kossuth March' therefore anticipated 'General Haynau and the Draymen', and it may be said that in this way the music hall was an instrument of education.

Such songs as 'General Haynau and the Draymen' had a necessarily short life. Cynically engineered to cater for an explosion of indignation, they were soon forgotten when the audience had found a new outlet for its wrath. Much the same applies to songs that hang too closely on a contemporary peg. The limits of 'The Exhibition of 1862' and 'The Calendar Polka 1884' are self-evident, and the 1877 song 'Zazel' would not convey much to those who have forgotten that she was a circus star fired from a cannon in Westminster Aquarium. 'Have you Seen the Shah?' was written when the Shah of Persia came to Britain in 1873, 'The Kiss in the Railway Train' was motivated by a court case in which Colonel Valentine Baker was ruined because he kissed a girl in a railway carriage, 'Chang, the Fychow Giant' mirrored the interest in a 7ft 8in man put on show at the

Westminster Aquarium ('The Aq'). 'Beautiful for Ever' was sparked off by the exploits of Madame Rachel who ran a beauty shop and an assignation agency, with that title as her motto.

'The Wizard of the North' recalls the conjuror John Anderson (1815-74) who did a series of exhibitions and shows under that cognomen, and the various gorilla songs ('Mr Gorilla', 'Gorilla Quadrille', 'Gorilla Polka') owe their inception to a day in 1876 when the first live gorilla was exhibited in London. The song writers had a double chance at gorillas; the first gorilla speedily died, but another was brought to London in 1879 and shown at the Crystal Palace.

In 1865 the Salvation Army was formed by William Booth 'for the evangelization of the very lowest classes'. The Salvation Army was always good for a laugh, and sparked off a number of songs such as 'The Hallelujah Band' and 'A Round-aboutish sort of

An audience queuing outside the Standard Music Hall in the East End, a hall that survived in the face of the opposition of the big music hall syndicates of the 1880s. Few great names, no lavish productions, but admission was only fourpence

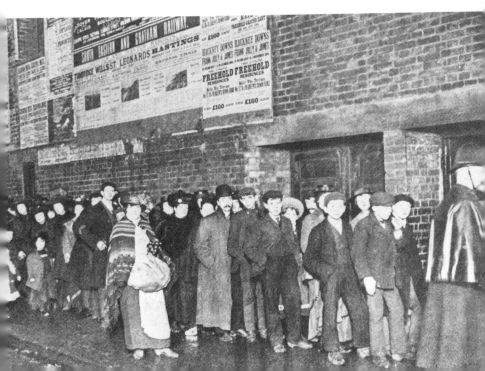

Way of Going to Jerusalem'. The established religion received very little coverage by the singers of comic songs, but unusual sects were fair game. Spiritualism had its commentator with 'Knock, knock, my ma's a medium'.

The Salvation Army had the last laugh. In 1882 it bought the Eagle Tavern and Grecian Theatre in the City Road, formerly the Royal Eagle Coronation Pleasure Grounds and Grecian Saloon that in 1838 had been a pioneer in popular entertainment and had paved the way for the music hall of 1848 and after.

The music hall audience appreciated the specific, both in locale and circumstance. London was changing rapidly. In 1870 the Thames Embankment was opened, and this event was good for a song, 'As I Strolled Along the Thames Embankment'. Belgravia, the suburb custom-built between 1826 and 1852, had many of the overtones that today surround the King's Road, Chelsea. 'Belgravia' was sung by Vance, and to amplify that Belgravia was the trendy place there came 'The Belle of Belgrave Square'. One of the happiest of songs relating to London was 'Hampstead is the Place to Ruralize', one of the wittiest 'Hornsey Wood, or I Really Think She Did'. These references reinforced the impression of togetherness, a feeling fostered also by the love and domestic songs that were invariably staple diet. Unlike the love songs of the drawing-room and parlour, the best of music hall were wry and ironical, self-mocking and sentimental:

When I first courted Nancy she was, oh, so very shy,
And when I kissed her first she broke my nose
and blacked my eye.

There is the surrealist inconsequence of:

Her front name is Hannah
Her father's a tanner,
But him she does hammer
In an artistic manner,
She sings 'Star Spangled Banner'
And 'Farewell Alanna'

With a toothbrush I fan her
When she thumps the 'Pianner'.

Or the complexity of:

I fancied her, she fancied me,
We fancied this and that,
And Nancy she would often say
Her heart went pit a pat;
But my fancy fancying,
For fancy it must be,
I thought I'd fancy Nancy
'Cause Nancy fancied me.

For the majority of the music hall audience, courtship was a
short bitter-sweet memory. Leybourne, Vance, and the lesser
lights, played lightly on this theme. Here is Leybourne:

Jemima she was a domestic,
With blue eyes and hair so dark,
The first time we met I'll never forget,
She was wheeling the kids round the park.
The sun it was rather oppressive,
So she sat down beneath a big tree,
I sat down as well beside that girl,
For I thought she was spooney on me.

In courtship there were recognized hazards:

'Twas late at night to see her, by Love's passion I was led,
I felt so disappointed when I found they'd gone to bed,
The window rose, her mother emptied something on my
head,
I was wringing wet through serenading Sara.

Such songs seem harmless enough, and it is astonishing that men
of the world such as William Hardman, lawyer and diarist, should
write: 'These infernal Music Hall songs are all the rage and a
fearful subject for contemplation such a fact is.' One gets more of
an insight when one reads the sly songs

I met a little charmer
  So did I,
And said I wouldn't harm her,
  So did I,
I took her into Short's,
And stood her wine by quarts,
  So did I.

And there is sauciness in these lines of Arthur Lloyd:

I kissed her twice upon her lips
I wish I'd done it thrice,
I whispered, oh, it's naughty,
She said, it is so nice.

Even so, Hardman's diatribe might be more comprehensible if we were acquainted with the exact content of the music hall song as it was sung and not as it appeared, bowdlerised, in sheet music or word book form. It is evident that on many occasions the singers, such as Macdermott, who was eventually barred from the respectable stage, not only extemporised extremely bawdy spoken business but took liberties with the verses and choruses of the songs as well. Innuendo was augmented by wink and nod.

The opposition to the music hall ethos also took exception to the fact that the Lions Comique treated marriage pragmatically:

Before I was married I'd a pocket full o' quids;
Now I've got a pocket full of holes and seven kids.
I ought to be the 'appiest individual on the earth,
But I've been a grumble-izer since my birth.
Just because the nippers scream and shout,
Just because the wife throws plates about,
Just because she beats me now and then,
I've come to the conclusion I am not like uvver men.

Even the sanctity of marriage was questioned:

When we get married, it ought to be understood
That man has the right to change his wife if she's no good.

This could work both ways, as we see from this 1880s song by Jenny Hill (known as 'The Vital Spark', famous for her Cellar Flap dance):

> He's out on the fuddle, with a lot of his pals,
> Out on the fuddle, along with other gals;
> He's always on the fuddle, while I'm in such a muddle,
> But I mean to have a legal separ-a-a-tion!

There is occasionally a ruthless touch totally alien to what is considered to be Victorian sensibility:

> Her salt tears notwithstanding
> He shoved her off the landing.

Yet for the true barb one must return to public subjects. In dealing with love, marriage, courtship, the singer knew that there was a line he must not cross. Homosexuality, perversions, queer practices, these could be delicately hinted at. The aesthetic movement provided material, but the references had to be oblique and guarded. In the public domain there were no such restrictions.

The power of the music hall is demonstrated by the case of Sir Charles Dilke. Dilke was one of the great politicians of the nineteenth century, diligent, immensely intelligent, and assiduous in a way few Victorian politicians were. In 1885 he married the widow of the eccentric Oxford don Mark Pattison, and in 1886 he was involved in a divorce case; 'with coarse brutal adultery more befitting a beast than a man, he was charged with having done with an English lady what any man of proper feeling would shrink from doing with a prostitute in a French brothel.' So said the prosecuting counsel Henry Matthews.

It is evident that there is a cruel streak in the music hall singer's treatment of marriage, a cynical streak in his treatment of war and foreign affairs, arousing in his audience a fervour that was often reprehensible. Macdermott read about the Dilke case, and his rabble-rousing instincts came to the fore. Here was a man being crucified in public; Macdermott added an extra nail.

Master Dilke upset the milk
Taking it home to Chelsea,
The papers say that Charlie's gay,
Rather a wilful wag.
This noble representative
Of everything good in Chelsea
Has let the cat, the naughty cat,
Right out of the Gladstone bag.

Dynamic and assured as the Lions Comique were, their lack of sensibility mars their stature. Their songs were cold and calculated and even with their uplift songs they inserted the occasional 'er' and 'um' to show that they themselves had reservations about the sentiments. They were professionals who had adopted a persona; but the persona overtook them. Their songs are the polar opposite of 'The Lost Chord' and ballads of that ilk.

They realised that to preserve their pre-eminence they had, to quote the words of one of their songs, 'to go the whole hog or none'. In doing so they lost some of their humanity, though they eclipsed the men of sentiment, such as Harry Clifton who could 'supply a want which has long existed, viz. a lively, merry ditty, that can be sung at a private family party, either by lady or gentleman, without the fear of offending propriety'.

The Lions Comique also outrank those who came later—Dan Leno, debut 1885, Albert Chevalier, debut 1891, or Charles Godfrey, exponent of what was known as the Hi-Tiddle-I-Ti Business. They were not in competition with the women. Marie Lloyd, born 1870, Katie Lawrence, Vesta Victoria, Bessie Bellwood, or Louise Sherrington—these brought a new element into the music hall. The brutality was expurgated, and the innuendo was demasculinized. The songs relied more on their content than on their delivery, and were inclining more to the general than the specific, robbing them of local colour but adding a universality that has kept them in the repertoire.

In place of the drive and pace of 'Champagne Charlie', the changes of mood and rhythm of 'The Excursion Train', the inbuilt obsolescence of 'Lounging in the Aq' (dead when Westminster

Aquarium was demolished in 1888), there is Katie Lawrence's 'Bicycle Made for Two' (1892), 'Our Lodger's Such a Nice Young Man', and the multitude of stage Cockney songs such as 'My Old Man Said Follow the Van'.

The world of Dan Leno, Albert Chevalier, Harry Hunter ('His Name Was Joshu-a' and 'I Saw Esau Kissing Kate') and Charles Godfrey was totally different to that of the Lions Comique. The 1878 Act demanding safety curtains and a clear break between stage and auditorium had changed the character of the music hall. Intimacy was lost in the mammoth theatres of the syndicates, and a mediocre song could not make its own way. Synthetic as the costermonger and Cockney songs of the later period may be, as spurious as the uplift songs of the 1860s and 1870s, there is no question that they stand up on their own as entities, that they do not demand extra projection (though that helps). They also have two vital qualities—warmth, and better tunes.

This is not to say that the tunes of the earlier music hall were all forgettable. 'The Daring Young Man on the Flying Trapeze', written to commemorate the trapeze artist Léotard who did an act at the Alhambra in the 1860s, was a popular between-the-wars waltz and can still be heard at off-peak times on Radio Two. 'Up in a Balloon, Boys', sung by Leybourne, is still in the repertoire, its contemporaneousness forgotten in the lilt of a pretty tune. But they have not acquired the status of urban folk song, reserved for the mock Cockney songs of the later artists or such charming offerings as 'Daddy Wouldn't Buy Me a Bow-Wow'.

It may be argued that the tunes of the late Victorian music hall are not better, that we have been brainwashed by nostalgia and by the wider coverage given to the late songs by the successors to Chevalier, that the mammoth figure of Harry Champion, with a delivery and gusto that matches those of the great figures of the past, has made such a mark on the genre as to obliterate the possible mediocrity of his material.

The song writers of the late Victorian music hall were, like their predecessors, poorly paid. George Le Brunn, who wrote the music for Marie Lloyd's 'Oh, Mr Porter!' was content with a guinea a tune, though the status of composer and lyric writer had improved since the days of Charles Sloman. In the 1840s and 1850s he charged ten shillings a song, while he was prepared to supply poems at the rate of five shillings for twenty lines, and threepence a line after. Many of the singers wrote their own songs, including Henry Sydney (died 1870) and Harry Clifton (died 1872), and to them the words were the all-important thing.

The tunes were scrambled together anyhow, adapted from popular quadrilles, waltzes, and polkas, pirated from other writers, or dredged from the folk-song repertoire. The uplift songs were doggedly four-square in structure, harmonically unadventurous; the comic songs had just enough tune to get by. The most important factor was making certain that the words could be distinctly heard.

It might be supposed that with the larger theatres of the post-1878 period the audience would have greater difficulty in catching the words of a song simply because they were further away from the singer. However, the Palaces and Hippodromes were better designed acoustically than the earlier music halls, many of which were adapted from existing buildings, and the provision of the Suitability Act in forbidding eating and drinking

Typical of the new music hall that followed the emergence of music hall syndicates in the 1880s was the Hippodrome, Nottingham, solid, lavish, and placed in a commanding position in the main square of the town

in the auditorium eliminated the clink of glasses and the clatter of plates.

The great boom in provincial theatres in the 1870s and 1880s also rendered obsolete the songs that relied too much on local references. Nobody in Birmingham was much interested in Belgravia, and Leybourne's 'Pride of Petticoat Lane' struck dully on Oldham ears. It was soon found that pseudo-Cockney was acceptable throughout the kingdom, and a talented band of composers and lyric writers rose to accept this challenge—Edgar Bateman with 'It's a Great Big Shame' and 'If it Wasn't for the 'Ouses in Between', E. W. Rogers with 'If You Want to Know the Time, Ask a P'liceman', Fred Gilbert with 'The Man Who Broke the Bank of Monte Carlo' and 'At Trinity Church I Met My Doom', and Joseph Tabrar with 'Daddy Wouldn't Buy Me a Bow-wow'.

To some historians of the music hall, the great age runs from the 1880s to the start of the first world war, and revivals of music hall rarely seem to go much earlier. Certainly the music of the later period wears better.

CHAPTER FOUR

BURLESQUE

IN 1831, ELIZA VESTRIS opened the newly decorated Olympic Theatre in Wych Street. It was the first time a woman had controlled a theatre, and she had a woman's intuition of what would go well. This was burlesque, and her first show was *Olympic Revels*, in which she herself took part, a type of early principal boy in breeches and close-fitting costume.

The actual construction of burlesque was loose, and the form included straight acting, straight singing, dialogue, comedy routines, and dancing. For more than half a century classical mythology, history, Shakespeare, operas and plays, and contemporary fiction, were plundered for burlesque, and although few of the pieces had lasting power, the ground was prepared for the Gilbert and Sullivan partnership and musical comedy. At its best, burlesque was a music hall evening compressed and with a plot. All things could happen, and the medium provided an incentive to the wits and satirists of the day, especially those who were associated with the humorous journals *Fun*, *The Tomahawk*, and *Punch*.

The writers were therefore mainly journalists, and as journalism at that time was fascinated by puns, copious and extravagant punning became one of the staple features of burlesque. Unlike the song and supper room entertainments and the music hall, the tendency of burlesque was towards the intellectual, and although the groundlings in the audience were feasted with colour and costume, the extreme cleverness of the song lyrics could easily pass them by.

Madame Vestris provided the locale, J. R. Planché provided the impetus, an unlikely source, as he was a bookish man and a scholar, in later life becoming Rouge Croix pursuivant of arms at the Heralds' College. When he was seventy-three he was requested by the War Office to arrange the collection of armour at the Tower of London in chronological order. Born in 1796, Planché, an Englishman despite his name, wrote his first burlesque

The Knight and Sprite was a burlesque by Gilbert à Beckett performed at the Strand Theatre in the mid-1840s. Burlesque, an amusing and under-rated art form, was a precursor of the Savoy operas of Gilbert and Sullivan

for Drury Lane Theatre in 1818, but his interest in light
entertainment ran parallel with his fascination for correct
historical dress. In 1823, for a production of Shakespeare's
King John, he designed the costumes; it was the first time that
historical drama had been dressed in the authentic manner.

When she opened the Olympic, Madame Vestris arranged for
Planché to write a series of plays, and for *Olympic Revels* he
produced the appropriate classical costume, as well as ensuring
that the mythology was reasonably correct. This preoccupation
with accuracy was a hallmark of Planché's work for the theatre,
and along with it went crispness and craftsmanship. He was a
good model for later writers in this field, and an 1840 invention
of his, Baron Factotum, Great Grand Lord Everything, was
clearly known to W. S. Gilbert when he came to conjure up
Pooh-Bah. Planché and Gilbert overlap; Planché's *Babil and
Bijou* dates from 1872, Gilbert's first burlesque *Dulcamara* 1866.

To give some idea of the quality of Planché's wit, here is an
extract from *The Golden Fleece* of 1845:

Jason: À la bonne heure—now, madam, you talk sense,
         I'm vexed you gave my friend the King offence.
         And as to Glauce—
Medea: Oh! Don't name that creature.
         I heard her say, 'If your wife bores you, beat her!'
Jason: You quite mistook her—the reverse meant she—
         Beta in Greek, you know, is *Letter B*.

The neatness of this double-pun is worth more than interment
in a passing burlesque, but the refreshing thing about the writers
for burlesques is that they were stimulated by the challenge, and
were not jaded by having to rhyme 'moon' with 'June'. The
literary factions of the mid-Victorian period did not consider it
demeaning to test themselves in the public forum. In a similar
way, superb graphic artists of the time, such as Leech and Keene,
found there was nothing tiresome in earning a living doing
cartoons for *Punch*.

Even the programmes of the burlesques are replete with
displays of exuberant punning. A parody of *William Tell* called

Tell! And the Strike of the Cantons has, as a subtitle, *The Pair, The Meddler, and the Apple*, and the character list include a mayor ('goes well in harness, quiet to deride or drive') a 'broth of a boy himself, but a *broth*-er of his sister Lisetta, consequently a *soup*-erior person', and the heroine, Emma, 'one of those eph-*Emma*-ra that brighten a husband's existence'.

The burlesques not only had a battery of clever writers. Actors arose who had a penchant for the form, the most prominent being Frederic Robson, a recruit from the song and supper rooms where he was renowned for his rendering of the Cockney monologue 'Villikens and his Dinah'. He brought such commitment to his work in burlesque as to transcend it. Henry Morley, Professor of English at University College, London, took time off from writing histories of English literature, to investigate the art of Robson. 'It is odd enough', he wrote, 'that at a time when all serious acting is tending to the burlesque and unreal, a

A tableau from the pantomime Cinderella performed at the Lyceum in 1844. Pantomimes and burlesques were expensively and lavishly staged, and were full of theatrical gimmicks

burlesque actor should start up with a real and very serious power in him'. The long-serving and encyclopaedic critic of the *Daily Telegraph*, Clement Scott, was equally enthusiastic. Robson's burlesque performances of Shylock and Medea 'were so desperately earnest; the real and the grotesque were so happily blended that those who sat astonished in the theatre did not know whether to laugh or cry'.

Although music was an integral part of the burlesque, it was never considered superior to the words. Frequently, following the pattern of the first and perhaps the best burlesque, Gay's *The Beggar's Opera*, old tunes were refurbished, such as 'Cherry Ripe', which would take new words without taking the attention from them. The typical role of music in burlesque is exemplified by the following extract from the programme of *Sisterly Service*, performed at the Royal Strand Theatre in 1860:

> In the course of the evening the Band will perform the 'Mazurka des Fleurs,' by F. Wallerstein, published by Metzler and Co., 37, Great Marlborough Street, where may be had the 'Tyrolienne', by the same Composer, danced by Miss Rosina Wright, in the Burlesque.

Among the major writers of burlesque were Shirley Brookes, William and Robert Brough, George Augustus Sala, F. C. Burnand, E. L. Blanchard, Gilbert A'Beckett, and Henry J. Byron.

Shirley Brookes (1816-74) was a genial, clever man, for many years on the staff of the *Illustrated London News*, contributing the weekly article on politics. During this time he was also writing burlesques, and in 1851, fortified by this experience, he joined *Punch*, writing his shrewd, laconic series 'The Essence of Parliament'. He became editor in 1870. He was noted for his astonishing memory and brilliant quips. William and Robert Brough were writers, two members of a talented family. Robert, who died young, was famous in his day for his satirical *Songs for the Governing Classes*, while William was on the staff of *Fun*, the humorous weekly that was started in competition to *Punch*.

George Augustus Sala was one of the finest journalists of an age that teemed with fine journalists. In his early days he did odd jobs

The burlesque at the Olympic Theatre in 1863

scene-painting in theatres and illustrating books, and his burlesques were side issues from being involved in theatrical pursuits. Dickens discovered him in 1851, using his work in his own magazines, and sending him to Russia in 1856 as a special correspondent. In 1860 Sala edited the magazine *Temple Bar*, but his time in Russia had given him a taste for world travel, and in 1863 the *Daily Telegraph* made him special foreign correspondent, sending him to cover wars in America, Algeria, France, and Spain. Trying to emulate Dickens by starting a magazine of his own, Sala failed lamentably, and he had to sell his library of 13,000 volumes. With his red, bottle-nosed face, Sala was one of the characters of the mid-Victorian Bohemian subworld.

F. C. Burnand (1836-1917) is rather sombrely enshrined as an editor of *Punch* for twenty-six years, but before he took over that role he was celebrated as the author of more than 120 pieces— farces, burlesques, opera librettos, and adaptations from the French. His best known burlesque was itself a take-off of an existing burlesque, *The Latest Edition of Black-Eyed Susan* (1866), which ran for two years, though in historical context his most important was *Box and Cox*, with music by Sullivan (1867), anticipating Sullivan's work with Gilbert and giving Sullivan a taste for the medium. Burnand was acquainted with Gilbert, both of them being in at the birth of *Fun;* Gilbert published his *The Bab Ballads* in *Fun*, and many of the verses from this extremely amusing series were served up later when he was collaborating with Sullivan.

E. L. Blanchard (1820-89) was known as the hero of a hundred pantomimes, and he too was associated with the early numbers of *Fun* and acquainted with the circle that met at the Arundel Club, where subjects for burlesque were broached and deals made. As a boy of seventeen he had been a reporter for the scabrous weekly *The Town*, and had never quite lived this down.

There were two Gilbert A'Becketts, father (1811-56) and son (1837-91), and both were prominent writers of burlesque. There is a curious link between Sala and the elder A'Beckett (who

The burlesque at the Haymarket Theatre in 1863

A superbly evocative engraving by 'Phiz' of an 1856 pantomime audience

naturally claimed descent from *the* A'Becket) for his burlesque *The Yellow Dwarf* was being produced when Sala was painting the scenery for this piece. The son enjoys a unique place in burlesque annals for burlesquing Gilbert. A'Beckett the younger was on the staff of *Punch* from 1880 onwards.

H. J. Byron (1834-84) was actor, theatrical manager, writer of burlesques and serious drama, and the editor of *Fun*. Although his burlesques have been attacked for their violence and for their witless punning, he acted as a useful catalyst, introducing Burnand to the Arundel Club and making him one of the charmed circle of burlesque writers. His addiction to the pun was with him to the end; on his death bed his groom reported the illness of a horse, and asked if he should give it a 'ball'. 'Yes', replied Byron, 'but don't ask too many people'.

This clique dominated burlesque writing for a generation, and it is not surprising that there is a family resemblance. If one browses through issues of *Punch* of the period one gets the flavour of these burlesques—reactionary, too full of word play, but clever.

This music/drama form was regarded as disposable, and although Planché had established a reputation for precision and accuracy, this was not shared by other promoters. The hundreds of burlesques that passed through the theatres gave audiences the taste for quick-witted dialogue; this was also being acquired by music hall audiences, newly attuned to the innuendo, the patter songs, the spoken business of the Lions Comique, and these trends were complementary, bracing the audiences and putting them on their mettle. The public clearly indicated that they liked this. It only needed someone to bring order into the chaos of burlesque, to channel the work of the writers and bring in new players.

John Hollingshead did this. A cloth merchant and a journalist, he started theatrical life as a stage director at the Old Alhambra, and took a lease of the Gaiety at the wrong end of the Strand. Music had been the poor relation in burlesque; anything had been good enough if it acted as a backing to the words. He altered this; over the years he produced forty musical burlesques at the Gaiety with a precision and a deftness that had so often been missing, and he had achieved this in part by recruiting players from the music hall. Burlesque had been the refuge of the stock actor out of a place, and by bringing in the music hall artist's timing and intention to be innately funny rather than merely speak the lines, Hollingshead scored a signal success.

He also provided his patrons with a full evening of entertainment, recognising that his audience was basically middle class and wanted value for money. His programmes opened at 7 o'clock with a straight drama, the burlesque began at 9.30 and finished at 11.15. By his championship of what he called the 'Aunt Sally of the critical press', Hollingshead made possible the Savoy operas of Gilbert and Sullivan.

W. S. Gilbert was acquainted with the other writers of burlesque, and from the inception of *Fun* was a regular con-

The Prince of Wales' Theatre in Tottenham Street, once renowned as a home of burlesque, photographed in 1900 shortly before its demolition. Like the Grecian, this theatre had been taken over for a time by the Salvation Army

tributor, though he failed to break into *Punch*, the then editor, Mark Lemon, seeing nothing amusing in the *Bab Ballads* (1861, put into book form 1869). His appointment as drama critic of the *Illustrated Times* turned his attention to the stage, and when a bright Christmas piece was wanted for the St James's Theatre in 1866, to be written in a fortnight. Gilbert was asked to do it, selling *Dulcamara* outright for £30.

The collaboration with Sullivan began in 1871, and extended well into the 1890s. So much has been written about this partnership, about the coolness over a carpet that nearly broke them up after *The Gondoliers*, about Sullivan's constant veering between comic opera and serious music, that it is unnecessary to go into it all again. Sufficient to say that *HMS Pinafore* (1878), *Patience* (1880) and *The Mikado* (1885) transcended burlesque, but that without the background of burlesque they could scarcely have existed. The Savoy operas were perhaps the most significant musical works produced in Victorian times.

Although Gilbert was the driving force, and although he himself devised rhythms for Sullivan to follow, the contribution of Sullivan was far greater than in the burlesques, being more akin to the work of Offenbach. Sullivan could burlesque serious music with a deftness and charm that is unequalled; recitative in *Patience* caricatures the recitative of Italian opera, and in *Iolanthe* there is a fetching parody of Wagner for the number 'With humbled breast and every hope laid low'. The Bach-style introduction to the Nightmare Song 'When you're lying awake with a dismal headache' echoes the sombre song and supper dirges of the 1840s, such as 'The Maniac', while the pseudo-Japanese touches in the music for *The Mikado* have precisely the right ambience.

Gilbert was a master of words and the Savoy operas are full of marvellous couplets:

Three little maids who all unwary,
Come from a ladies' seminary, *The Mikado*

When the coster's finished jumping on his mother—
He loves to lie a-basking in the sun. *Pirates of Penzance*

He could use verse to set a mood with as exquisite a touch as Tennyson:

When the night wind howls in the chimney cowls, and the bat
in the moonlight flies,
And inky clouds, like funeral shrouds, sail over the midnight
skies,
When the footpads quail at the night-birds wail, and black dogs
bay the moon,
This is the spectre's holiday—then is the ghosts' high noon!

The literary articulate environment of the Bohemian circles of mid-Victorian London was responsible for much that was good, providing a cool oasis in the frenzy of nineteenth century progress. That there was such an eager audience says much for the perspicacity and intelligence of that often maligned segment of society, the middle classes.

A musical comedy of the closing years of the century, illustrating the lavish sets and costume and large casts

Musical comedy was complementary to the later works of Gilbert and Sullivan, and was characterised by contemporary realism, especially in the costume and decor. The first musical comedy was *In Town* in 1892, and it was only a moderate success, but when *A Gaiety Girl* appeared in 1893 it was an unqualified hit. The libretto was written by Owen Hall alias James Davis, a solicitor and a journalist with a penchant for getting into trouble. He founded a scurrilous journal called *The Bat* and was sent to gaol for an article on a race-horse trainer whom he declared to be 'as hot as the hinges of hell'. Hall followed up *A Gaiety Girl* with *An Artist's Model*, *A Greek Slave*, and *The Geisha*.

The balance of musical comedy was tilting back towards the music, and the promoter of musical comedy in the 'nineties, George Edwardes, found the ideal counterpart to Hall in Sidney Jones, born in 1869. Jones composed a song 'Linger longer, Lucy, linger longer, Loo' which appealed to Edwardes so much that he signed up Jones to write the music for *A Gaiety Girl* and subsequent musical comedies. His tunes were catchy and memorable, and unlike burlesque where the music was secondary to the text, these could be extracted from the body of the work in a similar way songs from early Victorian opera were taken from the context (such as 'Home, Sweet Home').

Like the music hall, musical comedy provided material for the drawing room, and sheet music selections from *A Gaiety Girl* and *The Geisha* were sold in their thousands and tens of thousands. Success breeds success, and in 1894 *The Shop Girl* with music by Ivan Caryll was put on at the Gaiety Theatre, running without a break for two years, rocketting the Gaiety shares up from three shillings to a pound.

Ivan Caryll, real name John Tilkin, had studied in France as a singer and had come to London in 1882. With a view to making his musical comedies as full of plums as possible, Caryll did not hesitate to work with other composers on one work, two of whom were to make their mark in Edwardian musical comedy, Lionel Monckton and Paul Rubens.

Musical comedy of the 1890s ran in close harness with the new music hall, and the players were interchangeable. There were

Miss Kate Vaughan and Miss Nellie Farren, two celebrated music hall beauties

considerably more women performers than there were in the 1860s and 1870s; their principal contributions were pertness and sauciness, and they were naughty in the nicest possible way. The men were debonair and stylish, and there was little of the savagery and intensity that marked the Lions Comique. They were knuts rather than swells. The songs from the musical comedies could equally well have been written for the music halls; 'Tell Me, Pretty Maiden, Are There Any More at Home Like You?' would have been as much at home in the halls as on the musical comedy stage (it came from the musical comedy *Florodora*).

The mood of the 'nineties was reflected in both music hall and musical comedy. England was emerging from the repressions and the fug of Victorianism. After so many false starts, a new age seemed to be dawning at last.

CHAPTER FIVE

MUSIC IN THE HOME

IN EVERY HOUSE there is an altar devoted to Saint Cecilia, and all are taught to serve her to the best of their ability. The altar is the pianoforte. So declared *Chambers' Journal* in 1881, and around this altar music in the home revolved. The piano was a status symbol in the lower middle class home, a symbol that was augmented if it was effectively used, and hundreds of thousands of girls were set at the task of playing this instrument.

This destiny had been awaiting them since the introduction of Hawkins' Portable Grand Piano of 1800. The novel thing about this piano was that it was upright. It did not take up the inordinate amount of room of a grand piano, and although the cost did not enter into the calculations of John Hawkins, the construction of upright pianos proved cheaper than grands.

It was some time before the great pianoforte makers became aware of the possibilities of the upright. In 1827 the French maker Pleyel exhibited an upright piano, followed in 1831 by Erard. These were considerably lower than Hawkins's, which was in effect a grand piano on its side, and they led imperceptibly on to the twenty guinea cottage piano, adorned with fripperies, with silk-facings across intricate fretted fronts, which merged with the clutter of the middle class drawing room.

All young ladies with pretentions to gentility were expected to have some musical accomplishment, whether they were the daughters of bank clerks or the aristocracy. Girls of noble birth acted as Maids of Honour to Queen Victoria, who was fond of music and never forgot that she was taught by Mendelssohn. She had a light agreeable voice, and the summons to accompany her on the piano was not one that could lightly be disregarded. The hint was not lost on young ladies who occupied the Maids of Honour sitting room at Buckingham Palace, the furniture of which consisted of two writing tables, two armchairs, a round table, two footstools, two pair of silver candlesticks, a sofa, two cabinets— and a piano.

There were pianos too in plenty at the Queen's residence at Osborne in the Isle of Wight. One of the Maids of Honour in 1854 was Mary Bulteel, the niece of the Queen's private secretary, and she was pleased with her prowess at the piano compared with the other ladies of the court. 'Lady Ely', she wrote to her mother, 'is good nature itself, though her accompaniment is rather mediocre —no ear—so does not know when wrong basses are put down.'

The full attention of the audience at concerts and musical evenings was never really expected or demanded. A sketch done for the magazine London Society in 1865

Miss Bulteel had to make her abilities known—'Fancy my audacity at offering to play "Marie Stuart" when the Queen was walking away from the pianoforte.'

She was frequently asked to sing, but the Queen had her own ideas of what constituted a good song, and Miss Bulteel was not able to render her own favourites. There were risks as well—always the chance that Lady Ely would accompany her, and it needed a good deal of tact for the girl to keep the accompaniment in her own hands. There were also problems of etiquette; one night the Queen was going to sing duets with her Maid of Honour, but thought that this would disturb the whist party and asked Miss Bulteel to sing alone. To make matters worse, the Prince Consort was playing billiards. Miss Bulteel got through the ordeal well, and was complimented by the Queen.

In 1858 she was at Osborne again, and in the party was Lady Mount Edgcumbe who was 'such a comfort' in her accompaniments and duets. Lady Mount Edgcumbe thought highly of the young girl's talents, and gave her a batch of duets to look through. 'If I ever have to accompany them I shall die', she wrote, 'such difficult German music.' This difficult German music was more to the taste of the Prince Consort than the Queen, and although he tried to inculcate his wife in the beauties of Teutonic music, and was indeed a composer of moderate competence and an organist with a partiality for solemn improvisation, she preferred the homely and the well-known.

The fact that the Prince was a music lover, a patron of the Ancient Concerts (an organisation that had stumbled along for many years), and that the Queen adored him and went along with everything he did or believed, made music in the home more than respectable. It was a patriotic duty. The Queen invited the most famous musicians of the day to play before her, including Clara Schumann and Liszt, and the aristocracy felt compelled to do likewise—not necessarily the very top layer (for they had a custom of doing what they wanted when they wanted), but the minor members scrabbling for a place in the sun.

Many of these people were astonished that the performers whom they had invited to their houses to give recitals did not

The piano recital was not introduced into the public domain until well into the century. When the performer struck the public imagination, there was no limit to the acclaim. This cartoon of 1900 depicts Paderewski

appreciate the honour that had been accorded them. At one recital in 1856, Clara Schumann had the impudence to stop playing half way through a piece because the audience were chattering and would not proceed until they had stopped.

This happened to Mendelssohn, but knowing his place in the hierarchy, he solved the problem with tact and discretion. At one of his recitals before a jewelled audience, during the slow movement of Beethoven's 'Moonlight' Sonata, a stately dowager in the front row began opening and closing her fan to accompany each bar; the rustle and the click must have sounded as though the sonata was being accompanied by a dance-band drummer. Mendelssohn did nothing so startling as stopping. He merely repeated the one bar over and over again in time to the fan until the woman had seen the error of her ways and folded the fan up.

Such drawing room music was not meant to be fun. The nobility were following the lead set by Royalty, and were in their turn providing an example to their inferiors. Conversation at recitals was quite in order; how else was one to prevent being bored? It was even written into books on etiquette, the authors

The rapt attention of the audience in this illustration of the 1880s would have been welcomed by many budding pianists and violinists

Playing the piano was not only an aid to flirtation: there were perils, too

of which were on the very lowest rungs of the social ladder and desirous of pin money. *Manners and Tone of Good Society* laid down the form:

> When music is given at 'afternoon teas' it is usual to listen to the performance, or at least to appear to do so; and if conversation is carried on, it should be in a low tone.

Clara Schumann maintained: 'It is the artists' own fault: they allow themselves to be treated as inferiors in English society.' She was fortunate in that she was in England on a short tour, but musicians who lived in England were obliged to kow-tow to custom. The best and most accomplished of composers had to perform in private houses to eke out a living, and it was not until 1861 that public recitals were given, when Charles Hallé paved the way, though he had been giving piano recitals in his own house since 1850.

The quality of music in drawing rooms ran the whole gamut from the abysmal to the superb. At the Prinseps' house in

Holland Park there was frequently music of a high order. Val Prinseps was a painter associated with Rossetti and the Pre-Raphaelite painters, and the residents included the artist G. F. Watts. In June 1859, Hallé and the violinist Joachim played there. One of the guests was the Pre-Raphaelite sculptor Thomas Woolner:

> They played the pieces of Beethoven, and the indescribable agitation, the unutterable yearning reaching nearly death, then the pause, and then wild mad exultation of triumphant passion subsiding through sweet varieties into continuous tendernesses of melodious sound, were rendered in a way that made the listeners well believe that the instruments had vital souls.

Even when there were no professional musicians involved, drawing-room music could be demanding. In January 1876, Mary Gladstone, the daughter of the politician, was a guest at Hagley Hall, the Worcestershire home of the Lyttelton family. Miss Gladstone, then aged twenty-eight, was an energetic, not to say ferocious, music lover, a seasoned opera-goer and concert-goer, and a pianist of considerable ability. It is evident that there was a good deal of pleasure in the music-making at Hagley Hall:

> Concert at 8. Leapt up and down continually. Played the Moschelles (frightful) and the Freischutz (fair) . . . also the lovely Spohr Barcarole. Mrs Fennel played a *tour de force*, the Weber rapid end movement of a Sonata, in 3 minutes. Miss I. thundered out the Mendelssohn Concerto; we all ran away desperately in 'Tramp'. Mrs Glover Eaton sang 2 Ballads to perfection. Mendelssohn's D minor Trio rather feebly played, and a miserably childish set of Marta airs on the Cello completed the programme.

This was the Victorian musical evening at its best. Enthusiasm in plenty, a stimulating standard of performance, and the willingness to have a shot at something that may have been beyond the capabilities of the performers. Such evenings could be combined with other amusements. One of the daughters of the

Soul and intensity were demanded of the more lachrymose drawing-room ballads, as can be seen in this atmospheric engraving of the 1860s

house was Lucy Lyttelton, and it is clear from her Diary (7 October 1858) that there was nothing solemn about such evenings:

> For the evening came Mr and Mrs Duncome, and her two sisters, who made most beautiful music, singing Italian together in such harmonious unison, with full soft voices. There were also two comic songs, and to wind up, the most capital jig, performed by Lord Boyle and Cousin Bick.

The performance of music in such enlightened households was as natural as eating. This extract is again from Lucy Lyttelton's Diary (11 August 1858):

> Mr Girdlestone came for two nights, and we had a pleasant evening, combining words, poets, concertina, whist, reading and conversation.

A formal musical matinee of the mid-1880s, more of an occasion for showing off the latest fashions than a musical experience

It would have been inconceivable in such circles that people could actually view attendance at musical evenings as a chore. Clifford Harrison was one of a now lost species, the professional reciter, either solo or with musical accompaniment. One afternoon he was giving a recital at a private house in London, and sitting opposite him was a pretty woman:

> She preserved all through the recital the gravity of a South Sea idol. Eyes had she, and pretty ones—yet, metaphorically, she saw not; ears certainly were there, with a diamond in each—neat, shell-like ears too, but they were no indices of hearing. Vacuity sat enthroned on her charming face. Such steadfastness of purpose really amused me to watch. One wondered what world it was she was denizen of.

Only once did this woman come to life. During his rendering of Browning's 'The Pied Piper of Hamelin' he quoted the lines 'To see the people suffer so from vermin, was a pity.' She looked round at her friends with 'a sort of mute appeal and surprise, as of one who was not accustomed to hear such a word in society.'

Many other performers at twee *matinées* and *soirées* had this kind of experience. The numbers of the interested were generally exceeded by the talkers and the vacant; attendance was the thing, and not enjoyment, and some paid entertainers lowered their standards to get some response from the audience. John Hatton, whose 1850 song 'To Anthea' was once very popular, was an all-round entertainer, and one of the first to do 'songs at the piano' together with piano solos and humorous lectures. His audiences were 'moved with delight and excited with laughter'. His performances were assisted by his appearance; his head was 'like a boiled egg with a fringe round it.'

Clifford Harrison, the reciter, was not sufficiently exclusive for attendance at his recitals to be worth mentioning for months afterwards, but there was a small nucleus of celebrities whom not to have seen was social ignominy. These included the opera singer Jenny Lind, who had a great liking for the grand scene and enjoyed being courted by the upper classes, and Chopin. Chopin visited London in 1848, and played for the Countess of

The ideal music-room of the 1890s, sporting not only a new Chappell piano but an organ

Blessington at Gore House, Kensington (the Albert Hall was built on this site), and for the Duchess of Sutherland at Stafford House. These two society ladies held rival salons, and attendance at either of them merited a top score. Chopin also gave matinées at the house of Mrs Sartoris at 99, Eaton Place, and the house of the Earl of Falmouth, at 2 St James's Square.

These recitals were considered so important that outsiders were invited, such as music critics, and being present on these occasions carried with it immense prestige, especially as Chopin died the following year. The elite would have liked to have got their teeth into Liszt, but Liszt did not play for money after 1847.

In some of the great houses music was a ritual. At the Duke of Bedford's castle at Belvoir, summons to breakfast was carried out by the duke's private band which marched round the castle playing sprightly music. The same procedure was carried out for dinner, and as soon as the dessert was placed on the table, singers came in and diligently performed four pieces of music, two solos, and two ensemble pieces.

The popular conception of the Victorian evening was the lady who took her harp to a party and was not asked to play. The only thing wrong with this is that she would have been asked to play. Time lay heavy on the leisured classes, and it needed a lot of filling. Music of whatever kind was worth having as a background

The muted tragedy of a young performer being put on display before his time. The age was not strong in musical prodigies

ROUGH ON MUSIC.

Musician (ironically): "I AM AFRAID MY MUSIC WAS DISTURBING THE PEOPLE WHO WERE TALKING OVER THERE."

Hostess: "DEAR ME! I NEVER THOUGHT OF THAT. DON'T PLAY SO LOUDLY NEXT TIME."

A cartoon of 1899, reflecting a situation not far from the truth

to gossip and scandal. To be asked to sing could be a dread imposition as it was to the undergraduate John Bacchus Dykes, who was later to be a well-known hymn writer. Summoned to the home of the Vice-Chancellor of Trinity College, Cambridge, his first *faux pas* was to turn up in evening dress rather than academic costume. His second was to meet the eye of his hostess, and his fate was not averted by vigorous conversation with young ladies nearby. No doubt he wished that he could have been, in the words of his best-known hymn, 'Nearer My God to Thee.' However, he survived on a mournful drawing-room ballad. Most people did.

Reluctant singers or pianists were pleased when the noise of conversation obliterated their humble efforts. What was dreaded was the hush that preceded the song, the faint pain on the faces of the audience, the grimace from the hostess that promised a post mortem in one of those catty letters that bored, underworked society people were prone to write. Such a hostess in the 1850s and 1860s was Mrs Brookfield, the wife of a popular preacher, who pinned her guests for the benefit of her husband:

> Mesdames D., W., and M., with respective husbands attempted glees, accompanied by H., a faint bleating being all that was achieved.

Most guests were only too pleased to be asked to perform; amateurs have commonly a high opinion of their merits, and their aim was to still the buzz of conversation, to identify with Gilbert in Oscar Wilde's *The Critic as Artist*:

> And now let me play Chopin to you, or Dvorak? Shall I play you a fantasy by Dvorak? He wrote passionate, curiously-coloured things? . . . After playing Chopin, I feel as if I had been weeping over sins that I had never committed, and mourning over tragedies that were not my own.

To evoke the kind of response described in popular magazine fiction—this extract is from *Stone Steps and Wooden Stairs* by Beatrice Leigh Hunt serialised in *Cassell's Family Magazine* in 1874:

The stillness was an involuntary tribute to his power, while even those of his hearers who could not boast any keen perception or appreciation of the art of music were stirred by the pathos of this minor lament . . . No cough was heard, no undertone comments, for in that universal silence any breath of sound except the music itself seemed as if it would have profaned the quivering air.

Unfortunately for amateur musicians with soul, the Victorians could rarely be kept quiet except in church or at oratorio. They were the definitive running commentators, whether they were the lower orders in the music hall where their participation was welcomed, whether they were the middle classes gathered in drawing rooms for musical evenings, or the upper classes at the opera.

There was a formula for after-dinner music. The ladies departed from the table, the port and claret went round twice, sherry was offered, coffee was called for and the men joined the ladies, who split up from a cluster and flew to the most interesting men. Conversation took place, and a lady emerged from the melee who had a voice or a touch; she was not sure if she had brought her music, but her husband had done so, and it was in a portfolio in the hall. While he fetched it another gentleman had escortd her to the piano to turn over the pages, and while she protested that she was so out of practice she rapidly divested herself of gloves, fan, and handkerchief, which with a dexterity born of long experience she arranged on or over the candle brackets which were a decorative feature of the Victorian upright piano.

Thus prepared, the lady ran her hands up and down the keys with what was known as the 'butterfly touch' as a signal for conversation to cease, or at least drop in decibels. The audience stared at the ceiling, preparing their faces for melancholy or gaiety depending on the mood of the music. Execution was of less importance than touch or expression; a few wrong notes did not matter if the ones that were there were wrapped in sentiment. A fluttering tremolo was highly valued in singers, as this denoted sensibility.

Drawing-room musicians seen through jaundiced eyes, a curious engraving of 1885

'Such songs as "The Lost Chord" were accepted as test-pieces for tears', wrote E. F. Benson, the popular novelist. 'The singer tried her strength with them, as if they were punching machines at a fair which registered muscular force.' 'The Lost Chord' was written by Arthur Sullivan in 1877. It sold 500,000 copies in twenty-five years.

. Publishers who succeeded in reaching the drawing-room audience were certain of a rich haul. Enthusiasts would happily pay out four shillings for the latest ballad, and it was therefore understandable that the publishers laid out large sums of money on promotion, hiring or even building halls for ballad concerts at which their ballads would be relentlessly pushed. The response of the audience would determine how much effort would go into the promotion. Sometimes there was no doubt at all; 'The Lost Chord' was clearly a winner, and so was 'The Three Fishers', at the debut of which 'there was a tumult of applause; people rose

The roseate hues of early dawn,
The brightness of the day,
The glory of the sunset sky,
How fast they fade away!
Oh! for the pearly gates of heaven,
Oh! for the golden floor.
Oh! for the Sun of Righteousness
That setteth nevermore.

*The apotheosis of the drawing-room ballad, which was divorced from
everyday life and catered for a comfortable melancholy*

in their places and cheered, waving hats and handkerchiefs in their excitement'.

Victorian popular music reached a low with the drawing-room ballad. It was a dishonest medium, cajoling the listeners into believing that they were getting art music instead of a sticky mass of sentiment and tired melody. The most incredible thing was that the composers and lyric writers were equally certain that they were producing works of art.

Three of the most prolific writers of drawing-room ballad were John Blockley, J. E. Carpenter, and Fred Weatherley. Weatherley was asked how many songs he had written; he did not know. In one ottoman he had fifty-one volumes of eighteen to twenty songs each. Titled ladies were very strong on the production of drawing-room ballads, and, with their market in mind, they enjoyed a success that was hardly deserved. 'By the Shore' by Lady Lindsay was a slow dismal song, mercilessly savaged by the critics, who pointed out that the words 'by the shore' were repeated no less than nine times. In the market place it did not fare so well as 'In the Gloaming' by Lady Arthur Hill which sold 140,000 copies between 1880 and 1889.

The dreary mid and late Victorian ballad cannot be compared with the airs taken from the early Victorian operas by Balfe and Bishop. Superficial as they were, they were composed rather than concocted. It was the policy of Blockley to ransack the poetry of Longfellow and Tennyson almost before it was dry on the page, extracting fragments that would fit into a musical setting. Tennyson's 'The Charge of the Light Brigade' first saw day in a newspaper, and as it was written during the Crimean War, its topicality was immediately seen by Blockley. The men who had not gone to war would surely stand round the piano and bellow it out.

Typical of the lyrics of Blockley's songs were these, from 'The Better Land':

Is it far away in some regions old,
Where the rivers wander o'er sands of gold!
Where the burning rays of the ruby shine,
And the diamond lights up the secret mine.

THE·HOME·THAT·WAITS·FOR·ME.

WORDS BY MARY SIDWELL.

MUSIC COMPOSED BY M. W. BALFE.

Drawing-room ballads were published in weekly journals. 'The Home that Waits for Me'
with music by Balfe was an attempt to exploit the 'Home Sweet Home' market, but this
particular song was soon lost to sight

From Carpenter's output is the first verse from 'Sunshine and Cloud':

> Sunshine and cloud, love, Still there must be,
> Then if for others, Oh! why not for me?
> Bid me be happy, Oft as ye may,
> Thoughts will unbidden, Darken life's ray.
> Still when 'tis darkest, Light I can see,
> Thou art the sunshine, Beaming for me!

There is a melancholy strand running through the ballad form, judiciously selected for the easy tear. 'All Things Pass Away', 'poetry' by S. Pascoe, is representative:

> The dry leaves of Autumn, So yellow and sere,
> Last rays of the bright sun Decay of the year.
> The pale light the moon brings Last shadows of day,
> These teach us that all things Are passing away.

As in folk song, the ballad of the drawing room was deeply involved in lost loves. 'Rosaline' by J. H. Eccles was one ungathered bloom:

> From morn till night where'er I roam
> Thy form still fonder comes to view!
> Thy gentle falling tresses
> And eyes so soft and blue.

The archetypal drawing-room ballad can be simply constructed by linking together the songs of Stephen Glover:

> Voices of the Day
> Why do Swallows Change their Home?
> To the Woods! To the Woods!
> Light in the East is Glowing
> The Lily and the Rose
> All Things are Beautiful
> Where Shall We Find our Home?
> Where are the Flowers?
> Listen! 'tis the Wood-bird's Song
> Hark! I Hear the Organ s Peal!

Tell Me Where Do Fairies Dwell?
Tell Me Where is Beauty Found?
Say, Where Shall We Roam?
When Shall We Two Meet Again?

All questions, exclamations, and speculations attuned to the ethos of the drawing room, with melodies that kept stolidly to an easy level and a piano accompaniment that lay comfortably beneath the fingers—no difficult passages to afflict the pianist and cause the singer to sink in bathos instead of pathos.

The drawing-room ballad reflects its audience, which wanted a buffer against reality. Financially secure, it was yet full. of anxiety—anxiety about death, about sex, about the restlessness of the poor, increasingly stigmatised as the 'dangerous classes'. Drawing-room ballads served not only to pad out the long winter evenings, they were comforting, a solace in uncertain times. The overall tone might have been melancholy, but it was rarely tragic; sadness was invariably redeemed by a gleam of hope—the loved one might have gone, but there was a good chance that he/she would reappear, either in the not too distant future or in the Hereafter, which was looked upon as a repository of wish fulfilment, as exemplified in 'I Come From the Spirit Land', words by Miss Darling, 'a dreamy strain elegantly touching upon spiritual influences, and treated with the hand of a master.'

The publishers not only had popular material in the ballads as they were written; there was money to be made from the arrangements. An immensely successful song was 'Shells of Ocean' by J. W. Cherry. The narrator is walking by the sea shore, and picks up a few shells; he/she is thrown back into nostalgic memories, a child again, but throws them one by one away, for 'by toys our fancy is beguiled/We gather shells from youth to age/ And then we leave them like a child.' This was arranged by the publishers for two voices, three voices, voice and guitar, piano duet, flute and piano, concertina and piano, piano solo, and as a florid piano fantasia.

Although the music hall had its motto songs, such as Henry Russell's 'Cheer, Boy, Cheers', as devoid of individuality as the most vapid drawing-room ballad, it was in touch with reality. The early Victorian songs from English opera were tuneful. But even when the ballad composers took their text verbatim from English poetry, they rarely enhanced it, but degraded it and made it commonplace. It was not to the credit of celebrity singers of the time that they rushed on to the band waggon, sponsoring drivel because the chore was well-paid, bribed to insert new drawing-room ballads in their programmes.

Music in the home covered every kind of music from the worst ballad badly sung to out of tune pianos to masterpieces superbly played in perfect surroundings. The amount of music performed was incredible. It is surely better that music-making occurs, no matter the quality, than that it does not. Although we may question the merit of the drawing-room ballad, it served a useful function as a social integrator. The family that plays together stays together, and although we may shudder at the prospect of hearing 'Shells of Ocean' waveringly droned out by three timid daughters accompanied by maybe a flute, a concertina, and a piano, do-it-yourself music is an activity that we could have more of today.

The drawing-room piano was an aid to flirtation. This was the dream, but the reality was often far different

Music-making in the Victorian home fits in with the sociological pattern of nineteenth century life. The middle classes emulated what they thought were upper class leisure habits without quite knowing what these were. Middle class musical evenings had a note of forced gentility, and amateur performers who did not come up to scratch were considered to have let down their class. A summons to sing could be an ordeal, a circumstance that would have puzzled upper class habitués of musical evenings such as the Gladstone and Lyttelton girls.

Except when high-powered professionals such as Chopin or Joachim were recruited, formality was lax in aristocratic homes. Guests wandered in and out of the music room at will. The middle classes less often had a music room; their soirees and matinees were held in the drawing room, in which drawing-room behaviour was expected.

To some extent the middle classes were misled by the example of the Queen, who put a premium on formal entertainment, except when only her own family and intimate companions were present. In her attitudes and tastes the Queen was the quintessence of middle class mores.

Few generalisations can be made about music-making among the working classes, for this varied enormously depending on locale and the type of employment. Where there was a strong regional bias in favour of amateur music—in the industrial towns of the north such as Huddersfield or Leeds, or in South Wales— then the working population would frequently go short of necessities to provide themselves with the wherewithal to make music. Certain industries were conducive to music-making; the mills where brass bands were fostered implicitly encouraged music in the home, even if it was only to the extent of practising on cornet or trombone.

The piano was less in evidence in working-class music if only for the reason that, although pianos were cheaper than ever before, they were prohibitively expensive when the average working wage was less than £1 a week, though a lower middle-class clerk hardly earning more than this could go to any length to provide himself and his family with this precious status symbol.

Perhaps the most favoured instrument of the working people was the concertina, which was cheap and easy to play, not demanding any formal musical training. In middle class homes, the flute was highly thought of. This was considered a genteel instrument well suited to musical gentlemen. It had a plaintive melancholy tone in accord with the sentiments of drawing-room ballad and, a factor which put the stringed instruments out of court for many a household, the practising of the flute was not too irksome for unwilling ears. In this field, as in many others more highly publicised, children should be seen and not heard.

Despite its supporters' claims, the harmonium, looked upon today as the most Victorian of instruments, was never a threat to the popularity of the piano. Invented by Alexandre Debain in Paris in 1840, the harmonium, or portable reed organ, was received with a good deal of enthusiasm. It was ideally suited to religious music with its tremulous tone and sickly-sweet stops, but little music was written specifically for it and it was gradually accepted as a stand-in for the church organ.

Debain accelerated this by patenting the word harmonium, so that other makers had to invent other titles, such as seraphine, aeoline, melodicon, apollicon, and terpodion. It is often supposed that the American organ is a synonym for harmonium; however, it worked on an opposing principle. Instead of blowing air, it withdrew air. Nevertheless the sound is almost identical, and with the exploitation of the *voix celeste* stop the tone of the American organ was even more saccharine.

Harmoniums and American organs have the aroma of the mission hall always with them, though there is no denying that they suited the more plaintive and sentimental drawing-room ballads. Historically they are important in that they led up to the more spectacular use of wind forced through pipes in the huge orchestrions and fairground organs of the close of the century, though the true ancestor of these is the barrel organ.

CHAPTER SIX

MECHANICAL MUSIC

THERE IS ONE aspect of music in the home that has not yet been touched upon: what were lovers of music to do if neither they nor their family could play a musical instrument, and did not care for the rough and tumble of a musical evening with guest participation? Did silence reign?

Not necessarily, for the Victorians had access to a range of gadgets that produced mechanical music, the most important of which was the musical box. There were two kinds of musical boxes, the cylinder and the disc. The cylinder musical box, which was used throughout the whole of the Victorian period, was invented in 1796, when Antoine Favre of Geneva made mechanical music by fixing pins into the spring barrel of a clockwork mechanism, and screwing tuned teeth down so that their tips were played by the pins of the revolving barrel.

The original idea was to use this tiny, tinkling gimmick as an extra for snuff boxes and watches, but by about 1815 a number of watchmakers gathered together in Switzerland and began making larger musical boxes. These became more and more intricate and sophisticated, the barrels became larger, and by a clever arrangement of the pins a number of tunes could be put on one barrel. To increase the repertoire, a number of musical boxes were made in which the cylinders were interchangeable, and to vary the tone

*The cylinder musical box was one of the few means of hearing music in
the home without actually performing it*

refinements were added—tissue paper to give a zither effect,
repeated notes to emulate a mandoline, and the addition of drums
and bells gave a rhythmic counterpoint.

This continual improvement went on until about 1870, when
further development seemed impossible and all the changes had
been rung from the principle of a revolving cylinder flicking at
tuned pieces of metal. Although the manufacturers tried to
pretend that they were evolving new models, they were only
dressing up existing boxes, making the cases more gaudy, turning
the hammers that struck the bells into butterflies, appealing less
to the connoisseurs than the moneyed middle classes with a taste
for the garish.

The repertoire of the musical box altered with the changing
times, and with the technical improvements. In the early days
when musical boxes did not play terribly well the makers opted
for traditional tunes that everyone knew, but as the boxes became

THE PLEASURES OF FOLDING-DOORS.

Hearing "The Battle of Prague" played, with a running accompaniment of—One, and Two, and Three ;——and One, and Two, and Three ;——and · · · · · ·

A John Leech cartoon in Punch (1842). Leech himself was very susceptible to noise, and the ceaseless din of street musicians forced him to move house several times

better it was found that arias from operas, especially the more florid ones, transcribed well for the musical box, though not so spectacularly as operatic overtures. Italian opera was especially suited to the musical box, and as opera-goers belonged to the class that could afford to spend money on musical boxes—it must be remembered that up to the decline in the 'seventies they were precision-made and expensive—operatic arias and overtures proved popular.

Perhaps the most popular of all the tunes used for musical boxes was 'Home, Sweet Home', from Bishop's opera *Clari, the Maid of Milan* (1823), the epitome of drawing-room music. This was ideally suited to twinkling variation of a kind that the musical box could do so well. For those who considered that opera was the home of vice and sin, and that consequently the music was irremediably tainted, there were chordal arrangements of hymn tunes, and the passion for the oratorios of Mendelssohn and Haydn did not go unobserved by the makers, who cultivated the religious market by inventing a musical box and barrel organ combined.

Except to the most dedicated enthusiasts, the tone of the cylinder musical box is inclined to be monotonous. Limpid and clear, true, but the inability to hold long notes meant that there was a vast range of music that sounded ludicrous. The makers tried to turn this defect into an advantage by having a trill instead of a sustained note. The musical box was also deficient in carrying power. The essence of music in the home was that it did not prohibit that favourite activity, conversation, while the music was playing, and when two ham-fisted young ladies were banging out piano duets or a pale copy of a Lion Comique was bellowing forth 'Up in a Balloon, Boys', the most scandalous gossip could be exchanged without fear of being overheard.

When the musical box was performing, general conversation obliterated the sound. As a background to a quiet evening at home the musical box was ideal. It could run for a considerable time on one winding, and the absence of dynamics was an asset rather than otherwise. However, there came a time when the tunes on one musical box became intolerably boring. Interchangeable cylinder

A state concert of the early 1870s. Although the audience included French and Russian nobility, the fare offered here is the ubiquitous 'Home Sweet Home'

boxes were rare and prohibitively expensive.

The successor to the cylinder musical box solved the problem of a low sound level and small repertoire. In 1886 Paul Lochmann of Germany designed a musical box which would play a disc rather than a cylinder. The principle was the same—a series of notches on the disc flicked tuned teeth, and because the sounding board area was much greater the music was much louder. Disc musical boxes were either upright or flat; the upright ones were monsters, as tall as ten feet, and even the flat table models emitted far more sound than the cylinder musical box.

At first cardboard discs were used, but these soon wore out, and it was decided to use metal discs, which were strong, cheap, and almost indestructible. It did not take long for the possibilities of the disc musical box to be seen. In 1889 two major German firms began the production of this amazing invention, Symphonion and Polyphon, and although an American company began producing their version of the disc musical box, these two German firms dominated the European market, and great quantities began flooding into Britain.

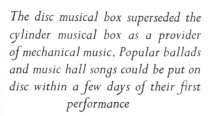

The disc musical box superseded the cylinder musical box as a provider of mechanical music. Popular ballads and music hall songs could be put on disc within a few days of their first performance

The obvious advantage over the cylinder box was that there was no limit on the repertoire. All kinds of music could be produced at short notice, and a music hall song that seemed to have possibilities could be transcribed to disc almost overnight. Public house owners realised that here was a way of not only having loud popular music permanently on tap, but of making money beside. Numbers of Polyphons and Symphonions were fitted with a penny-in-the-slot mechanism, and not only in public houses. Hotels and public rooms saw that these instruments were not only large and imposing pieces of furniture but were crowd-drawers, while private owners had the ultimate in status symbols, a disc musical box combined with a grandfather clock in the hall.

If the cylinder musical box reduced music to a norm, this was even more true of its noisy rumbustious successor, which reflected its period with a jangle instead of a tinkle. For those with a nervous temperament it must have seemed the last straw; it was the strident inescapable street-piano come indoors. For some kinds of music the disc musical box was ideal; it might have been designed for gay extrovert music, for the mock-Cockney ditties of the late Victorian music hall, for the lilt of Gilbert and Sullivan, for the tune-packed newcomer to popular music, the musical comedy, for the marches of Sousa, and for the wealth of popular nationalistic music. Other music fared less well. Hymn tunes such as 'I Know He is Mine' by Sankey, weepies such as 'Memories of Galilee' by Palmer, the mechanical piety of such music was given a surrealist tweak by the relentless oak creatures in the corner.

The barrel-piano and the barrel-organ had brought music to the lowest levels of society, those out of touch with even the most squalid music halls, and the disc musical boxes in the public houses carried on this worth-while tradition.

With the introduction of self-changing disc musical boxes, it would seem that the ultimate in mechanical music had been reached, but despite the advantages over the cylinder musical box, it was still only an approximation to the real thing. Historically, the disc musical box was dead almost before it was

Although the phonograph had been invented well before the end of the century, its possibilities were never realised, except in cartoon strips such as this from Cassell's Saturday Journal, 1899

born, for in 1877 Edison had invented the phonograph, followed
by Graham Bell's graphophone (1885) and Emile Berliner's
gramophone (1887). That these could be used for the trans-
mission of music was not realised for many years, and the nearest
approach to entertainment were 'Mr. Edison's talking dolls'
of 1890 which uttered about thirty words by means of a con-
cealed phonograph and clockwork. It was inconceivable that the
phonograph and its contemporaries could kill the disc musical
box, but they did, though the moment of truth was postponed
until 1914 when Polyphon and Symphonion shut up shop, their
last ditch stand, a combination of disc musical box and phonograph, having failed.

Although the two kinds of musical box were the most prominent producers of mechanical music, there were a number of
mechanical organs made which operated by means of a perforated paper roll. The principle was as simple as that of the
musical box; the paper roll passed over organ pipes, and where
there was a hole in the paper an aperture opened and sound
came forth. These organs could be small—such as the Organette
of 1878—or large—such as the Orchestrion of 1887, and like
musical boxes could be tricked out with all kinds of super-
numerary gadgets, triangle, snare drum, bass drum and the like.

The small organs activated by a paper roll were popular in
church circles, where their plaintive sound was a viable alternative to the harmonium, but they were basically an American
product and have the aura of mission halls in the far west.

An eccentric variation on this theme was the Tanzbar
mechanical accordian of the 1890s, and even more way out
were two paper roll activated instruments patented in America
in 1894, the mechanised banjo and zither. If nothing else, these
three instruments illustrate the immense ingenuity that went
into the invention of mechanisms that would play music without
human agency beyond the turning of a handle. Whether it was a
hunger for gadgets rather than a hunger for music is a moot
point.

To many people, all these producers of mechanical music,
from musical boxes to self-playing accordians, were second best

Towards the end of the century, mechanical music became more and more spectacular. This orchestrion was decidedly a rich man's plaything

to the prime drawing-room instrument, the piano, and it was logical for manufacturers to try to think up some method of devising a self-playing piano. The fact that after a series of false starts they succeeded says much for the ingenuity of nineteenth century technology. However, it was not the British who were first with the automatic player-piano, nor the French, who had done even more to develop the modern piano, nor the Germans, with their great name for piano manufacture, but the Americans, who produced the Angelus player-piano in 1897. Like the Organette, this worked on the principal of a moving perforated music roll. In 1898 the Pianola made its appearance, and in 1900 the Apollo, and although the French had patented a player-piano activated by music rolls in 1863, the Americans were the first to make reality of a dream.

It is interesting to speculate what would have happened had the player-piano been evolved earlier. There were certainly no technical barriers to an earlier birth. The probability is that attention was too much concentrated on other methods, in particular the mechanical piano of M. Debain of Paris (died 1877). Debain took as his starting point the barrel-piano principle, but instead of a pinned cylinder he used a pinned series of planks, called planchettes.

To an ordinary upright piano, Debain supplied a second set of hammers working from above, set in motion by iron levers, the top ends of which projected as 'beaks' through a four or five inch comb. Into this space five octaves of the keyboard were compressed. The planchettes were set in a grooved route, and by turning a handle were moved along over the comb, the pins activating the projecting ends of the levers, which in turn operated the hammers against the piano wires. By having the pins of different lengths the inventor could determine soft and loud, and even accent.

The amazing thing about this far-fetched invention is that it works, but from the infrequency of their appearance it does not seem that there were great numbers of them imported into the country. Unquestionably a factor that worked against their success was the extremely inelegant *modus operandi*. Standing up and turning a handle on top of a piano was hardly lady-like.

This *piano mécanique* was a logical development from the barrel-piano, but whereas there were in the 1880s 400 barrel pianos in the streets of London, there were probably only a dozen or two

The amusing history of a popular song

pianos mécaniques in the home. The lack of success may well have deterred piano makers from making further forays into the field of self-playing pianos.

One occasionally sees these planchettes in antique and junk shops, the owners plainly puzzled by these pieces of wood two feet or so in length with pins sticking from them. The great advantage of the mechanical piano over other forms of mechanical music was that, in theory at least, long pieces of piano music could be played without break. It was just a question of keeping the conveyor belt of planchettes moving.

What is evident is that the Victorians were fascinated by the prospect of having music in the home without having to play it. They were unfortunate in that the basis of their technology was mechanical. Without applied electricity their inventors did the best they could; the musical box represented the most refined and sophisticated use of clockwork imaginable.

CHAPTER SEVEN

THE TONIC SOL-FA MOVEMENT

IT WAS THE aim of the middle classes of the Victorian age to improve the condition of the working classes. The upper classes did not much care either way. It seemed at times that the working classes were incorrigible and did not want improving, and that there was only one way to get at them—through their children. At a lecture given in 1837 at the London Mechanic's Institute, the educationalist W. E. Hickson said that it was his aim to have music taught to the youngest children, to improve their general taste—if necessary, forcibly. Music, he claimed, weaned the mind from sensual and vicious indulgences, and inclined the heart to kindly feelings and just and generous emotions. Nobody thought to ask him how he knew.

The establishment took the hint: children must be taught music. But how? The children of the poor were obviously too stupid to understand musical notation, and besides the teachers did not understand it either, and anyway it was a long-drawn out expensive business. And why waste money on a fringe pursuit which may ennoble children but would not help them in their subsequent careers up chimneys or down coal mines?

The Tonic Sol-fa system was music education on the cheap. Its place in a book on Victorian popular music lies in that despite its depressing middle class patronage, it persuaded many people

The Tonic Sol-fa singing system was instituted partly to instruct the working classes in music and to keep them out of the gin-palaces. This illustration of the mid-1860s demonstrates that this cheerless task— for all concerned—outlived the first flush of enthusiasm

to take up singing for pleasure.

Fortunately there was on the scene at the time the very man to evolve a system that would wean the mind from vicious and sensual indulgences, John Hullah. Born in 1812 and receiving no musical education until he was seventeen, Hullah had no traumatic musical experiences to deter him from a venture into the unknown. He had studied singing for a time, and had become acquainted with Charles Dickens, with whom he wrote an opera, *The Village Coquettes*, produced at St James's Theatre in 1836

THE TONIC SOL-FA MOVEMENT

with scant success. Two more operas, *The Barbers of Bassora* (1837) and *The Outposts* (1838), were soon consigned to oblivion.

These failures encouraged Hullah to change his direction, and he began to investigate the teaching of music without using music notation. This had been done in Paris by Mainzer, but when Hullah went to see him, Mainzer's classes had been dispersed and he had been replaced by a man named Wilhem. So Hullah studied his methods, returning to England in 1840 where he made the acquaintance of the secretary to the Committee of the Privy Council on Education, Dr Kay, who persuaded him to promote the Wilhem system in Britain.

Hullah, a failed opera composer, needed little prompting, and within a few weeks he gave his first class lessons in Battersea. A year later he opened at Exeter Hall a school 'for the instruction of Schoolmasters of Day and Sunday Schools in Vocal Music', and had published, under the aegis of the Committee of Council, an English edition of *Wilhem's Method of Teaching Singing*.

It was believed by those opposed to Hullah's methods that Exeter Hall was underwritten by the government, but the money to run it came from the pupils themselves, mainly schoolmasters anxious to obtain diplomas, and from leading educationalists. Hullah's success was crowned in April 1842, when 1,500 people, mostly adults, sang at a great choral meeting. By that time Hullah was running courses at various levels. There was an Upper School, opened in December 1841, as well as the elementary school.

Hullah was at pains to stress that the Exeter Hall regimen was both Christian and socially integrated. 'Our meetings', he wrote in *The Duty and Advantage of Learning to Sing* (1846), 'include many a family circle entire—husbands and wives, brothers and sisters, parents and children; and these, in many instances, taught by one another.' The pupils were a cross-section—'clergymen, lawyers, doctors, tradesmen, clerks, mechanics, soldiers, and, of course, many schoolmasters and schoolmistresses.'

During the years 1841-43, the Exeter Hall teaching school made £1,122 profit, but this was siphoned away in other projects forced on Hullah by the Committee of Council model drawing,

Exeter Hall, which was one of the two concert halls existing in mid-Victorian London. Hullah took over the Exeter Hall to promote his Sol-fa system of musical teaching

arithmetic, writing, and chemistry—and on rent. St Martin's
Hall in Long Acre was built in 1847, and by 1850 had 1,400
pupils. Again Hullah maintained that there was no class distinction here. 'The pupils belong to every class and calling', wrote
an enthusiastic reporter of *Household Words*, 'the highest ranks
of the aristocracy, the members of almost every trade and
profession, the industrious mechanic and workman; and they all
mingle in one common pursuit, without regard to station or
degree.' It may not be a coincidence that *Household Words* was
run by Hullah's friend, Charles Dickens.

Nor is it odd that *Household Words* made no mention of rival
systems. Hullah was the chosen hero of the educationalists, and
why should a friend point out that the Hullah system of music
teaching had one major defect? Furthermore, a defect that was
not present in the rival system of John Curwen?

At this stage it might be pertinent to answer the unspoken
question 'What *is* Tonic Sol-fa?' Briefly, this is the substitute
of syllables for notes on a conventional music stave. In any key
there are seven notes. In the key of C, C D E F G A B were sung
as doh, ray, me, fah, soh, lah, ti, the subsequent doh being C
an octave above the original C. This is all very well for music
that is in the key of C, and does not fluctuate into a key where
accidentals are used. If the key modulates to G, an F sharp is
necessary; if the key modulates to F, there needs to be a B flat.

The major defect of the Hullah system was the fixed Doh. Doh
was always C. All Hullah's music was therefore cramped by this
limitation; all his music had to be transposed to the key of C.
John Curwen's system used a movable Doh; in the key of D,
Doh would be D; in the key of F sharp Doh would be F sharp.
However, this still did not solve the problem of modulation. In
simple music there was no need to use accidentals. Folk songs
were quite capable of being sung to the Tonic Sol-fa notation,
but in any music that was at all significant, or was in the minor
rather than the major, notes that were not in the original key
were bound to exist.

The remedy for this was to inflect the syllable that caused the
inconvenience. In the key of C, G is soh. So (pronounced *say*)

and si (pronounced *si*) would indicate to the singer whether the
G should be sharpened or flattened. But this destroyed the
simplicity of the system and most teachers preferred commonplace tunes that avoided the difficulties of modulation.

Below are extracts from two period music hall songs
'The Man Who Broke the Bank of Monte Carlo' and 'The Honey-
suckle and the Bee' with Tonic Sol-fa notation. The first song
keeps in the key and therefore there is no problem about applying
Tonic Sol-fa. In the first bar of the second song the vocal line
goes out of the key with a B natural instead of a B flat. This
problem is solved by altering the intonation of fah (marked f here),
the fourth syllable of the sequence doh, ray, me, fah, soh, lah,
ti, doh, to fe. The key is given before the Tonic Sol-fa notation
starts, and, of course, in this piano transcription of a song the
top note of the treble is the vocal line. The letters and numerals
beneath the bass stave are chord symbols.

Like Hullah, Curwen had not invented Tonic Sol-fa; he had
learned it from a Miss Sarah Glover of Norwich in 1840, who had
evolved it with a religious usage in mind, and although Curwen's
method was intended for promoting musical education in
Sunday schools, many teachers and authorities preferred it to the
more rigid Hullah system, and both systems were in use through-

The opening phrases of two popular songs with their Tonic Sol-fa notation

St Martin's Hall was built to provide Hullah with a permanent hall for his singing system. Completed in 1850, it had a seating capacity of 3,000

out schools and colleges, the particular method used depending on the whim of the teacher.

The Inspectors of Schools went from establishment to establishment, and by 1867 they had come to the conclusion that the Tonic Sol-fa system of Curwen was the one that should be adopted. In 1872 the government decision to make vocal music a compulsory subject in schools gave added impetus to the Curwen system—unfortunate for Hullah as 1872 was the year he was made Chief Inspector of Training Schools.

Although 25,000 people had passed through his hands between 1840 and 1860, Hullah had had major setbacks. His appointment as organist to Charterhouse in 1858 did not recompense for the burning-down in 1860 of St Martin's Hall. When he became Chief Inspector of Schools, Hullah was magnanimous enough to state that his own system should not be forced on to schoolteachers (though he considered it was still the best, and did his best to promote it, to the indignation of the Curwen school who considered that a Chief Inspector of Schools should be, like Caesar's wife, above suspicion).

Hullah did no good to the cause of popular singing by his continued advocacy of an exploded method, creating confusion where there need have been none. Curwen's son was carrying on his father's crusade; in 1882 he told an audience of educationalists that 80 per cent of all music teaching in elementary schools was carried out using his father's method. In 1853, 2,000 people were learning to sing by the Curwen method; by 1863 this had jumped to 180,000.

Curwen senior died in 1880, Hullah in 1884. Hullah had had a chequered career. His operas had failed, but his songs had succeeded. His early song 'The Storm' was a favourite of music hall audiences and 'The Three Fishers' was endlessly and obscenely parodied, a sure token of esteem. In 1876, out of sheer love of fun no doubt, the University of Edinburgh had conferred on him the honorary degree of Doctor of Literature. Hullah's *The History of Modern Music* (1862) hardly deserves that.

Both Curwen and Hullah were preoccupied with the ethical values of music. Curwen was an ardent temperance enthusiast, an aggressive dissenting clergyman, with fervent followers such as Henry Coward, strong on building up choral societies. The organ of the movement, the *Tonic Sol-fa Reporter*, called for sane minds in healthy singing bodies, and its articles frequently flitted off the subject of music to indulge itself in tirades against Sin and Low Dresses (the two, to the readers, being identical).

'Shall the Tonic Sol-faists?' asks the magazine. 'fall into the vortex?' Naturally not. Their training under the eagle eye of Curwen and Co. saw to that. Pupils who had had to cope with minor scales, the crux of all non-notational music systems, would have no difficulty with the demon drink, low dresses, and dancing in the streets.

There are indications that to Curwen Tonic Sol-fa was as much a moral discipline as a musical. His son made this clear in his biography of his father:

The method was the indirect means of aiding worship, temperance, and culture, of holding young men and women among good influences, of reforming character, of spreading Christianity. The artistic aspect of the work done by the Sol-fa method is indeed less prominent than its moral and religious influence.

Perhaps it was unfortunate that Charles Kingsley was not better acquainted with Tonic Sol-fa:

> I used to know only melancholy songs. I wandered about moaning in one eternal minor key. In heaven we shall sing involuntarily.
>
> (letter dated September 1843)

It is a pity that neither Hullah nor Curwen had any doubts at all about the efficacy of their various systems, both musically and spiritually. The Reverend Haweis, an odd musical gossip with a passion for violins, met Hullah, who claimed 'that if you go through the length and breadth of the land, you will find that the national ear has been to a great extent cultivated.'

All the Sol-fa systems were restrictive and crude. The choirs that sprang up with such enthusiasm could, at a pinch, cope with the classical works of the past such as *The Messiah*, but the lack of flexibility of music systems that ignored Staff notation was a barrier to the assimilation of the more modern music, increasingly chromatic and more adventurous harmonically. The Tonic Sol-far system was better able to cope with the milk-and-water religious music, and in a sense it was partly responsible for the welter of unimaginative works produced during the second half of the nineteenth century.

The wealth of Catholic music was perforce cut off from the Tonic Sol-faists, being not only unsuitable musically but suspect on religious grounds. Therefore the masterpieces of ecclesiastical music emanating from Catholic countries, such as Verdi's Requiem (1874), were forbidden territory, even to those who wished to enlarge their musical experience. Curwen objected to Protestants singing the *Ave Maria*.

He also had doubts about respectable folk singing glees and

part songs. These too often proclaimed the love of ale and the merits of a pretty girl. The accent was therefore on easy works with irreproachable sentiments, Sunday school music at its most depressing. Surprisingly, the Tonic Sol-fa system did not kill the relish with which northern choirs dealt with their chosen music, and it seems that the method musically succeeded while the noncomformist ethos behind the leaders was left behind on the way.

The Tonic Sol-fa system, with its concentration on the numbers of pupils who had 'passed' and on statistics, was unquestionably behind the new theory of choirs—that they should be large rather than good. The pinnacle of achievement—if achievement it was—was the Crystal Palace festival of 1862, in which 3,625 performers were gathered together under one roof.

Perhaps the greatest error of the Tonic Sol-faists was in assuming that their system was complete in itself. Had it been considered a stepping stone to ordinary musical notation, then one would have had nothing but praise for it. Dr Stainer (1840-1901), Professor of Music at Oxford, found 'that those who have a talent for music soon master the Staff notation after they have learnt the Tonic Sol-fa, and become in time good musicians.' The implication is that those who don't, don't.

The impression that the devotees of the various systems give is that they were sweeping the board, that the new schools brought into being by the coming of education for all in 1871 automatically took up Hullah or Tonic Sol-fa. The actual figures for 1880-81 are revealing:

School Board Schools (England and Wales)
ie schools brought into being by the Act

By ear 4,681	Hullah system 86	Tonic Sol-fa 1,414

Other Schools
(England and Wales)

By ear 17,470	Hullah system 628	Tonic Sol-fa 1,278

Schools in Scotland

By ear 1,280	Hullah system 8	Tonic Sol-fa 1,648

It will be noted that the only place where Tonic Sol-fa was really dominant was Scotland.

From the figures issued by the Tonic Sol-fa College, founded in 1869, it would seem that schoolmasters and schoolmistresses were conspicuous by their absence. In 1879-80, 15,755 certificates were issued by the College, and between 1869 and 1884 the total number of certificates was well over a quarter of a million. The original intention of the Tonic Sol-fa system, that it was to be the handmaiden of musical education in schools, seems to have foundered. One is thrown back to the notion that the institution that really profited from Tonic Sol-fa was religion, though unquestionably many middle-class and aspiring working-class people who laboured under the belief that conventional musical notation was difficult to learn took advantage of the College, too, and duly collected their certificates for framing in the parlour. Herbert Spencer the philosopher confessed that his love of music rose from his participation in Tonic Sol-fa.

A system, of course, is only as good as its teachers. Victorian teaching methods were, especially in the elementary schools, atrocious. The teachers were of poor quality, sandwiched in the class structure between the clerk and the shopkeeper. They preserved the illusion that ordinary musical notation is difficult to teach and impossible to learn.

One blessing of the methods was that music became cheaper. A Tonic Sol-fa edition of *The Messiah* sold 39,000 copies, and drawing-room ballads with Tonic Sol-fa notation as well as what musicians called 'the dots' helped to subsidise piano and instrumental music.

It is probable that Tonic Sol-fa did more good than harm. It instilled a love of music into children, men and women who otherwise would have had no knowledge of it. It provided a cadre for the many amateur choirs, especially in the north of England. To the more persistent it provided a stepping-stone to 'real' music. It was socially beneficial, and did keep many, as the *Tonic Sol-fa Reporter* claimed, 'from the dangers of the theatre, the snares of the dancing saloons, and the dissipation of drinking shops '

Professional musicians were more sceptical of its grander claims, and when they did praise it, it was qualified. Humdrum music was written with the limitations of Tonic Sol-fa choirs in mind. It was to the advantage of musical life in England that the system did not get the stranglehold on schools and on the working and middle classes that its devisers had hoped for. One wonders how many of the Working Men's Society, formed in 1867 for the performance of modern music, especially Wagner and Liszt, were graduates of the Tonic Sol-fa College.

CHAPTER EIGHT

THE PROMENADE CONCERTS

THERE WAS NO demarcation in Victorian England between popular and serious music, and the listener who wiped away a tear after a stirring performance of a drawing-room ballad was quite willing to stir himself for a Beethoven symphony. The idea of combining serious and popular music in one programme was in tune with the times, and was brought to a fine pitch by Louis Jullien, impressario, composer of dance music, and conductor.

At the time of Victoria's ascension to the throne, music was being diligently promoted, not merely as a pleasure but as a refined accessory to the good life and a help in moral rehabilitation. In 1835 George Hogarth, composer, 'cellist, and journalist, wrote *Musical History, Biography and Criticism*, in which he says:

> The diffusion of a taste for music, and the increasing elevation of its character, may be regarded as a national blessing. The tendency of music is to soften and purify the mind. The cultivation of musical taste furnishes to the rich a refined and intellectual pursuit, which excludes the indulgence of frivolous and vicious amusements, and to the poor, a *laborum dulce lenimen*, a relaxation from toil, more attractive than the haunts of intemperance.

This passage is a key to Victorian music between 1837 and 1850, and although Hogarth's view was shared by many people of influence, notably his father-in-law, Charles Dickens, the attempts to further it were either misguided or lacking. Instead of subsidising public concerts of good music, and encouraging musicians by patronage, music was either left to its own devices or byeways or was pursued with a diligence that was not warranted by the end result.

Among the things that could have been done but were not was the construction of concert halls. The Philharmonic Society was forced to mount its concerts in unsuitable places, such as the King's Theatre in the Haymarket, or the admirable but small Hanover Square Rooms built in 1774. The theatre was no home for the symphony concert; but was it suitable for concerts that combined serious and popular music?

The theatre managers thought so; they were aware that there was an unspoken demand for good music, and the song and supper rooms and taverns had demonstrated that the new urban public was interested in more than comic singers. The theatre managers looked to France. France had showed the lead in promoting ballet, which was now beginning to have a phenomenal success on the London stage, and since 1833 Paris had been enjoying promenade concerts under Philippe Musard, the key features of which were the mixture of all kinds of instrumental music and solo spots by virtuosos on newly evolved instruments such as the cornet-à-piston.

In 1838 the Lyceum put on such a promenade concert. The seats of the auditorium were boarded over to hold a standing audience, and an orchestra of sixty performed overtures, quadrilles, waltzes by such masters as Strauss and Lanner, and instrumental solos. The sceptical, considering that the low admission price of a shilling would bring only the riff-raff in, were astonished by the success of this concert, and it became a regular thing.

By 1839 other enterprises were going, including promenade concerts at the Crown and Anchor Tavern which included symphonies in the programme, and at Willis's Rooms, a superior

Until 1875, the Hanover Square Rooms were the premier concert rooms in London. Until redecoration in 1862, they were notoriously dingy, dirty and ugly, and no credit to the London musical scene

kind of dance hall, the Hanover Square Rooms, the Colosseum, a grandiose neo-classical building in Regent's Park, and the English Opera House. This sudden outburst of orchestral concerts created employment for the large number of musicians normally only active during the opera and Philharmonic Society's seasons, and although the concerts featuring symphonies in their entirety faded, it seemed that Londoners could not have enough of this new treat.

The standards of performance were extremely high, the soloists were expert, and great excitement was caused when it was announced that the Paris founder of promenade concerts, Musard, was coming over himself to give concerts. The Exeter Hall shareholders, hearing that Musard was hoping to rent their hall, refused to allow such jollification. The Exeter Hall was built solely for religious purposes; a year or two later they decided, however, to let rooms to John Hullah and his vocal system.

The public was sated by this exposure to full-blooded instrumental music, and by the beginning of 1840 it seemed that the capital could only accommodate one series of promenade concerts at a time, that the enterprise in the tavern saloons was doomed, and that audiences would only tolerate the better type of music if tantalised with noisy quadrilles and flashy waltzes.

This challenge was met by the Drury Lane Theatre, who brought over Louis Jullien from Paris, and from 8 June 1840 to 15 August, Jullien and his associate Eliason gave a series of promenade concerts under their French title *Concerts d'été*, with an orchestra of a hundred plus twenty-six singers. The promoters set the scene well; there were fountains playing and the auditorium was replete with flowers and growing shrubs, traditions kept up until the present day. Jullien ignored the failure of the promenade concert venture that put on symphonies, and as the concerts at Drury Lane went from success to success he added more meat to the programmes, performing Beethoven's 1st, 3rd, 5th, and 6th Symphonies; the latter, the *Pastoral* Symphony, he enlivened by having dried peas rattled in a tin box to give authority to the storm movement.

After the summer season was over, it was decided that the run must continue, and theatres that had dropped promenade concerts renewed their interest. The winter concerts at Drury Lane did not have Jullien, but instead Musard from Paris. Those who saw no good in importing French charlatans to give the common people music that was above their heads sniped at Musard, with his unseemly arrangements of tunes from Handel's *The Messiah*, and a Grand Overture by the Prince Consort, seeming to indicate that the Queen's husband had been drawn into this vortex, 'attracted neither notice nor applause'.

In January 1841, Jullien reappeared at Drury Lane, with bands off-stage and marvellous displays of trombone and cornet playing. The cornet player was rapidly becoming a star in his own right. This was Koenig, later to compose the celebrated *Post Horn Galop*, a must for every brass and military band of the last century. A season of German opera cut short this series, but in July, Jullien was back again in a newly decorated Theatre Royal,

Drury Lane. The decor included sculpture, including 'Eve at the Bath', and more and better flowers, fountains, and shrubs.

Jullien was being true to his public; admission prices were still kept within the reach of the man in the street. However, he was commercialising his talent. The quadrilles and waltzes which he composed himself especially for the promenade concerts were now being published in large quantities, and he was soon to start his own publishing and music-selling business.

He was also incorporating extra-musical items in his concerts, and a quadrille, 'de Vénus' was played 'with five Tableaux vivants'. In lesser circles *tableaux vivants* degenerated into strip-tease, but not with Jullien, for even though it only cost a shilling to get into his concerts there was never a hint of impropriety.

When he was not conducting concerts in London, Jullien was not idle. There were provincial tours to do, balls and parties to officiate at, and composing. Topicality and a change of programme were important. He was also a player of skill, and as he worked himself into a frenzy on one of his Monster Quadrilles, he would seize a violin or piccolo to add to the din of the climax before collapsing in an elaborate velvet chair. Showmanship could take precedence over the music; when he conducted Beethoven he used a jewelled baton and white gloves, presented to him on a silver tray.

There was a Welsh Quadrille, with a performer on a genuine Welsh harp, an English Quadrille, with ten fifes, a Scotch Quadrille, introducing the sound of a bagpipe. A piece extracted from Bellini's opera *Il Puritani* (a favourite of the Queen) was scored for twenty cornets, twenty trumpets, twenty trombones, twenty ophicleides and twenty serpents. Yet in 1846, Jullien had played at one of his concerts a work of such refinement as Beethoven's Violin Sonata, the *Kreutzer*, and no matter that the Septet was performed by more than sixty players, it was still Beethoven's Septet; Jullien's performance of Beethoven's Fifth Symphony was faithful and convincing despite the accompaniment of four brass bands.

The venues for his concerts changed from time to time, but no matter where he went Jullien triumphed, until in 1847 he tried his hand at opera. Opera was much in vogue at the time, and a second opera house in London was being opened to counter the monopoly of Her Majesty's Theatre. Jullien engaged Berlioz as conductor, and Sims Reeves, making his first appearance in opera, as male lead. The chosen vessel was Donizetti's *Lucia di Lammermoor*.

Hector Berlioz, whose works had failed to make any impression in Britain, despite the fact that he was the most adventurous composer alive, seized upon the appointment with joy. 'Art in France is dead', he wrote to a friend, 'and one must go where it still lives'. He was to receive 10,000 francs as conductor, plus another 10,000 francs for the expenses of four concerts, and a commission to write an opera for the second season.

Although *Lucia di Lammermoor* was a success, the mock-Scotch of this opera was not like the mock-Scotch of the Scotch Quadrille. Opera could not be meddled with, could not be backed up by rabble-rousing devices. Worst of all, they were much longer. The composer Balfe had had a great hit with *The Bohemian Girl* of 1843, and no doubt Jullien thought that he was on to a winner in commissioning Balfe to write another opera, *The Maid of Honour*, but not only was the opera not completed in time, but when it was produced it failed. The absence of a performable opera by Balfe forced Jullien into hurriedly improvised programmes, and an attempt to produce Meyerbeer's *Robert le Diable* in six days was traumatic to all concerned. All the participants became disillusioned, and there was a shortage of money. Jullien was judged to be bankrupt and in April 1848 his house at 76, Harley Street, was seized.

Jullien had been bankrupt in France, and being bankrupt in London did not dampen his spirits. He set forth again on another series of promenade concerts, in which he included one of the most advanced pieces of music of its day, Berlioz' overture *Le Carnaval Romaine*, and embarked upon a number of Monster Concerts (400 players and three brass bands). A Roman March by the Belgian bandmaster Bender included in its scoring twenty trumpets, especially made in London, that were nine feet long.

The academic world, resenting the success of Jullien when

'proper' symphony concerts were languishing, found much to cavil at at these concerts. Why, it asked, was Beethoven's Fifth Symphony played with scoring for four ophicleides and a saxophone (the critics probably meant a saxhorn)? And what was this nonsense that Jullien was putting over as music? (Berlioz' *Harold in Italy* for viola and orchestra, an undisputed masterpiece)

The Great Exhibition of 1851 might have been organised for Jullien's express benefit. He did not arrange to have five organs playing simultaneously at the Crystal Palace for the benefit of the Queen, but it is the kind of thing he would have liked to have done. His Great Exhibition Quadrille was written for 207 executants, and appealed to all, 'be he purist or gent-like' declared the *Illustrated London News*. Not surprisingly, the academic musical world determined to keep Jullien out of the exhibition jollities, and at Her Majesty's Theatre there was a renewed attempt to set up a rival series of promenade concerts. Instrumental in these was Balfe, no doubt still smarting under the failure of his opera.

Nevertheless the competition did not worry Jullien, and the new promenade concerts failed, lacking a conductor with the charisma of Jullien.

The Great Exhibition had brought forth a wealth of new instruments, including the guitarpa, a mixture of harp, guitar, and violincello, with thirty-five strings. This was a non-starter, though several new wind instruments by Sax were viable and were used by Jullien in a new series of concerts, plus an improved grand piano by Erard of Paris.

Once again Jullien made a rash venture into the quicksands of grand opera, and his own *Pietro il Grande* was produced at the Royal Italian Opera at Covent Garden on 17 August 1852. His mentor had been Francois Fétis, musicologist and composer, and director of the Brussels Conservatoire, whose operas were, states Grove's *Dictionary of Music and Musicians*, feeble and antiquated, and whose mass of church music was mainly unpublished.

Fétis confessed that he had been surprised when Jullien had

approached him for lessons in operatic composition, but Jullien had proved a willing pupil, though it is doubtful whether Fétis advised three military bands (one mounted) and a regiment of cavalry as essentials to the successful opera. The staging of this opera cost Jullien £16,000. 'It is wholly unnecessary to say anything more of that specimen of vulgar pretension than that it was most deservedly hissed off the stage', wrote J. E. Cox in his *Musical Recollections* (1872), though no doubt it was no worse than the Duke of Saxe-Coburg's opera *Casilda*, produced the same year at the Royal Italian Opera.

In 1853, Jullien went to America with his players, taking with him a repertoire of 1,200 works and a massive reputation, and during his absence other conductors tried to steal some of his territory, without much luck, and when Jullien returned in October 1854, it was as though he had never been away. A curious item on one of his concerts foreshadows a phenomenon of today, the scratch orchestra; in Pantomime Quadrille it was the duty of the orchestra to sneeze, snore, gape and laugh. But there was still Mozart, Beethoven and Mendelssohn in plenty.

1856 was a year of disaster for Jullien. On 5 March, Covent Garden Theatre was burned down. The celebrated conjuror Anderson, the Wizard of the North, was playing there, and there was considerable public interest in the fact that he had been playing at theatres before when they burned down. The Theatre had housed Jullien's repository of manuscript orchestral parts, and all were destroyed.

His second misfortune arose from his involvement in the Surrey Garden Company. The Surrey Zoological Gardens had been established in 1831, and it became a multi-purpose entertainment centre on the Vauxhall model, housing a menagerie, panoramas featuring Vesuvius and the wonders of Iceland, accompanied by fireworks, and other amusements. The concert hall that was to be the central feature of the new scheme, and Jullien's appointment as Director of Music and Conductor, seemed to spell opulence. An inauguration festival from 15-19 July included symphonies of Beethoven, Mozart, Haydn and Mendelssohn, Handel's *The Messiah*, and a Wagner overture. All seemed to be well with the Surrey Gardens, and in 1857 another mammoth festival was introduced, featuring oratorios by Haydn and Mendelssohn. There was a Rossini festival and a Verdi festival, but it became apparent that all was not as prosperous as it seemed. The receipts were being filtered away, the artists were not being paid, and Jullien was advancing money to stave off collapse though he had not himself been paid. He lost £6,000.

Temporarily subdued, Jullien made a comeback in the autumn, and began to prepare for a Universal Musical Tour, to carry music throughout civilisation. Before he went, there were a series of *Concerts d'Adieu*, the main item of which was his *Hymn of Universal Harmony*, the sentiments of which were not shared by his creditors, for before the triumphal tour could be carried out he was forced to flee to Paris, where creditors of long-standing were waiting for him. He was flung into a debtor's prison, tried to commit suicide, and died, aged forty-eight, a 'cosmic A' passing through his ears.

Who was Jullien, this incredible man whose impact on nine-teenth-century instrumental music cannot be over-emphasised, who introduced Berlioz and Wagner into the repertoire when established musical opinion fought shy of them, who made such endearing works as the overture to *Zampa* and *Raymond* familiar to the man in the street and made them compulsory entries into almost every brass band and military band programme?

What is known of the early years of Jullien is subject to doubt, and a brochure prepared for the American tour casts a rosy glow on his juvenile exploits. It is possible that he was in both the French navy and the French army, and he was certainly the son of a bandmaster; it is equally certain that his time at the Paris Conservatoire was undistinguished, even there more concerned with quadrilles than counterpoint.

Cherubini, the aged arch-priest of the Beethoven tradition—indeed, his own work is difficult to distinguish from Beethoven—considered that Louis Jullien showed promise, but under Jacques Halévy, a successful composer of light opera, he did not prosper, and when he left the Conservatoire in 1836 he im-mediately took up the cause of light music. When he was dealing

A concert at the Crystal Palace in the 1850s, shortly after the building was moved to Sydenham from Hyde Park. This drawing shows the type of seating used and the large

with the public his touch never faltered, whether it was in Paris, London, or New York; his introduction of classical music into his repertoire was masterly. First of all, a tuneful easy movement from a symphony to gull the audience into a sense of security, gradually an increase of dosage until the shilling promenader could accept an entire symphony of the classical period, then the casual insertion into the programme, alongside quadrilles and waltzes, of novelties by Berlioz and, later, Wagner.

Sir Thomas Beecham had a habit of inserting what he called 'lollipops' into his programmes, paralleling the dance tunes of Jullien's day. They were conscious bribes. Jullien could do this, but without condescension. To him, music was music. He saw no lack of respect in adding extra instruments to a Beethoven symphony or rattling a tin of peas to simulate a thunderstorm. Music was fun, and he made certain that his audiences agreed.

His departure left a gap in English musical life, and it was decided to carry on promenade concerts using exactly the same methods as Jullien, a crafty medley of good music, showmanship, and lollipops. August Manns, musical director at the Crystal Palace, was the first man to emulate Jullien, and he too included his own light pieces in his programmes, and in 1860 a fairly undistinguished conductor chose the Floral Hall at Covent Garden as his venue. Alfred Mellon's concerts lasted until 1866.

Jullien's son came to London in 1863 to take up the mantle of his dead father, but he was a pale copy and soon disappeared into obscurity. In 1865 a series of promenade concerts was given in which one conductor officiated for the serious music, another for the dance music, but the gusto imparted to the proceedings by Jullien was lost. The Alhambra music hall tried its hand, though concerts were soon discontinued, but in 1873, concerts at the Covent Garden Theatre recaptured some of the magic of the past.

In vain did the promoters employ big orchestras and accompanying military bands. Although Wagner nights attracted big audiences, the shilling promenaders were enticed away by rival attractions such as the big brash music halls. The promenade concerts tended to be watered-down classical concerts, and in

The nineteenth century offered more scope to professional musicians than previous ages, whether it was in the orchestra pit, the concert hall, or accompanying new ventures such as roller-skating, which enjoyed a great vogue in the 1870s. The participants circled the rink to lancers, quadrilles, and other popular dances

1893, after many flagging tepid years, the promenade concert seemed to be an extinct entertainment.

In 1895 the first conductor with personality since the death of Jullien appeared on the scene, Henry J. Wood, and he propelled the promenade concerts to fresh triumphs. But it was a different kind of concert. Jullien's programmes were forgotten, and so was the vivacity with which quite ordinary quadrilles were invested. The visual exuberant presentation was no longer there. There was, indeed, no substitute for Louis Jullien.

There was no Jullien to promote orthodox classical music. The Ancient Concerts, nominally patronised by the Prince Consort, were casually conducted and the music was indifferently performed. The Philharmonic Society concerts had a wide range of conductors, some of them good, some of them wretched. The latter included Henry Bishop, 'courageous to temerity in changing, adding to, and otherwise transmogrifying music committed to his care.'

The indifference of the fashionable public to anything new acted as a deterrent to adventure. In 1853, Schumann's Overture, Scherzo and Finale, received a first London performance; the music critic of The Athenaeum, a magazine noteworthy for its leaden spirit of reaction, considered it 'a display of unattractive cacophony' and approved of the audience's reception of it—received 'with the almost dead silence of disapproval.'

In the mid-century there were only two halls in London suitable for concerts, the Exeter and Hanover Square. The Exeter Hall management were very particular as to who hired the hall. The situation altered when piano manufacturers built halls to promote their pianos. The leading firm was Chappell, who built St James's Hall, and inaugurated a series of Monday popular concerts (the 'Monday Pops'). But these concerts were only popular in comparison with those of the Philharmonic Society or the Ancient Concerts and because the good music was leavened out with Chappell-published ballads.

Jullien had demonstrated that there could be an interest in classical music. Events proved that it could not be taken neat. The National Concerts never got beyond the prospectus stage,

The Queen and Prince Albert at a performance of Mendelssohn's oratorio St Paul at
Exeter Hall in 1845. It is clear that the Queen is of more interest to the audience than is

and gatherings of musicians anxious to stimulate serious music invariably failed. The longest-lived of these was the Society of British Musicians, which lasted from 1834 to 1865, achieving little. The New Philharmonic Society founded by Dr Wylde was a step in the right direction, but was handicapped by the founder being conductor from 1858-79 (Wylde was an academic composer/conductor of the worst kind). As if conscious that Dr Wylde was an incubus, members of the New Philharmonic Society founded the Musical Society of London, but their performances were mainly for their own amusement.

Chamber music was never even remotely popular, and although the Quartet Association was founded in 1852 by four executants of the highest quality, the best chamber music was to be heard in private homes performed by talented amateurs with the occasional guest celebrity.

Had Jullien lived longer he might have given chamber music the fillip it needed. The inclusion of the *Kreutzer* sonata in a promenade concert indicated his belief in public taste. Whether it was justified or not is a matter of opinion.

CHAPTER NINE

ORATORIO—PLEASURE OR PIETY?

IT MIGHT BE supposed that to include oratorio in a book on Victorian popular music is to stretch the term popular music too far. Yet oratorio was popular for a number of diverse reasons: it made people who went to oratorio feel highly moral and religious without the boredom of sermons or hymns; it was an excellent stamping ground for choral societies; it provided employment for operatic singers out of season; familiarity breeds content in music, and there could be nothing more familiar than *The Messiah*.

Oratorio is defined by the *Encyclopaedia Britannica* as a form of religious music with chorus, solo voices and instruments, independent or at least separable from the liturgy, and on a larger scale than the cantata. Although the formative years of oratorio were closely bound up with opera, by the time of Mozart it was moving towards church music, and although there is a chasm between the B minor Mass of Bach and the Handel oratorios they all encouraged a feeling of spiritual well-being in their audiences.

Handel brought oratorio to a fine pitch of perfection, and except for curiosities such as Schubert's *Lazarus* (1820), there is little of consequence between Handel and Mendelssohn. To the

Victorians, oratorio *was* Handel and Mendelssohn, and although newcomers such as Spohr's *Fall of Babylon* (1843) received an enthusiastic reception, they only momentarily interrupted the pattern.

Oratorio as exemplified by Handel and Mendelssohn fitted in with the early Victorian theory that, to quote the Reverend Haweis, 'music is not intended simply to tickle the ear; music means Morals'. *Elijah* was the finest example of this phenomenon, a grand compendium of significance:

> The novelty of treatment, the startling effects, the enchanting subjects, the prodigious daring of some of the situations, the heavenly melodies which have since become musical watchwords, and, above all, the presence of the composer, who sent an electric thrill through the room, and inspired chorus, band, and singers with the same lofty enthusiasm which made him so great and irresistible in achievement.

Oratorio appealed to Haweis and all his contemporaries, who insisted in reading into music non-musical qualities, who considered that music had a message that had escaped the composers and the more mundane listeners, an attitude of mind well put by Charles Kingsley in a letter of 16 July 1842:

> The great Mysticism is the belief which is becoming every day stronger with me that all symmetrical natural objects, aye, and perhaps all forms, colours, and scents which show organisation or arrangement, are types of some spiritual truth or existence, of a grade between the symbolical type and the mystic type.

The essential appeal of oratorio was put by Herbert Spencer the philosopher, a rationalist who had no religious axe to grind. He tried to analyse 'the emotion produced by sacred music,' as a 'sense of combined grandeur and sweetness.'

Even a no-nonsense girl like Mary Gladstone, daughter of the Prime Minister, felt that oratorio had to be treated with awe, as we see from this extract from her diary, 17 March 1877:

To the Messiah. No words can possibly describe its effect upon me . . . It is all-absorbing, takes entire possession of your whole being—it is divine . . .

It would be sacrilege to look at *The Messiah* as one looked at a symphony or other non-sacred work, though admittedly some did, especially the aristocracy, which reserved its fervour and quasi-religious adoration for opera (again full of non-musical metaphysical significance). The aristocracy not only resented the oratorio but the people to whom it appealed the most—the

Studies made during the 1874 Handel Festival at the Crystal Palace

middle classes, and especially the religious middle classes. It was an article of faith with the upper classes that all music worth the name was foreign music, and no one with an English background was worth taking seriously as a composer. Typical of this mode of thought was Lady de Grey:

> For English composers and English singers she had no sympathy at all—she thought of them vaguely as people who wrote and performed oratorios in cathedral towns.

Jane Welsh Carlyle was equally cool about oratorio and the oratorio mentality. She went to her second oratorio in May 1856. It was *The Messiah* and it left her 'calm and critical' on her rather hard bench. Her companion was Geraldine Jewsbury (1812-80), the writer of half a dozen forgotten novels. Miss Jewsbury told her that her sister Maria (1800-33) would not let her go to *The Messiah* when she was a girl because 'people who really believed in their Saviour would not go to hear *singing* about him.' Mrs Carlyle whole-heartedly concurred with this:

> I am quite of the religious Miss Jewsbury's mind. Singing about him, with *shakes* and white gloves and all that sort of thing, quite shocked my religious feelings—tho' I have no religion. Geraldine did a good deal of *emotional weeping* at my side. . .

Mrs Carlyle looked at the chorus with a degree of asperity, considering that she had never seen such a set of ugly creatures 'packed there like herrings in a barrel, into one mass of sound.'

The sense of the ridiculous that was such a strong feature of Mrs Carlyle did not infect other members of the audience. The audiences of the nineteenth century did not mind a static presentation; the first production of Gounod's *Faust* was done in a form that closely resembled that of oratorio, and so profound was the effect of the oratorio stamp that when Saint-Saëns' Biblical opera *Samson and Delilah* (1877) was presented in England it was as an oratorio, a shortcoming that was not noticed until 1910, when it emerged in its full lavish colours as a crowd-drawing opera.

In the age of massive choirs, the Crystal Palace was a Mecca for all those devoted to oratorio

The oratorio form conferred respectability on works that would otherwise have been still-born, such as *Eli* (1855) and *Naaman* (1864) by the composer/conductor Michael Costa, and many other English composers tried to jump on the band waggon, ransacking the Old Testament for obscure themes, though it became increasingly clear that the oratorio public preferred the old and familiar, confirmed by the amazing figures of the Handel Festivals at the Crystal Palace of 1857, 1859, 1862, and 1865, attended by more than a quarter of a million people.

The oratorio gave the music-going public a taste for choral works, and without that stimulus it is doubtful whether many admirable enterprises, such as the Royal Choral Society, would have succeeded. An audience nurtured on Handel and Mendelssohn oratorios were more inclined to attend a performance of Verdi's Requiem—first performed by the Royal Choral Society in 1875—than the average concert-goer, and choirs kept going by the repeats of the standard oratorios were able to provide a cadre for perhaps the finest choir of the period—the Bach Choir called into being for the 1875 performance of the B minor Mass.

The appeal of oratorio did not falter throughout the nineteenth century; its public was stolid and four-square, like the music, not given to fashionable caprices. To write an oratorio was to arrive. In 1889, 'The Oratorio is to the Musician the exact analogy of what the Cathedral is to the Architect —the highest Art-form to the construction of which he can aspire.' (*Grove's Dictionary of Music and Musicians*). It was a noble cause. The writer carried his analogy further; only the finest and the most moral of composers should write oratorios. 'Think what our towns would be, were builders of villas permitted to set up a Cathedral at the corner of every street'.

That so many excellent composers should have fallen for this trick is evidence of the powerful pressures brought to bear by the middle classes, the prime supporters of oratorio. These composers included the woefully neglected Sterndale-Bennett, a fine musician in the Mendelssohn tradition, who wrote *The Women of Samaria*, Charles Villiers Stanford who interspersed workmanlike orchestral works with *The Three Holy Children* (1885) and *Eden* (1891), and Alexander Mackenzie with *The Rose of Sharon* (1884).

The constant strain of writing in the *religioso* style acted as a dampener on professional composers, and people who loved music found the adulation heaped upon the arid note-spinning of oratorio too much to bear. When Bernard Shaw became music critic of *The Star* in 1888, he found the close-knit brotherhood of the oratorio composers suffocating. Writing of Stanford's *Eden* he went on to say:

Who am I that I should be believed, to the disparagement of eminent musicians? If you doubt that *Eden* is a masterpiece, ask Dr Parry and Dr Mackenzie, and they will applaud it to the skies. Surely Dr Mackenzie's opinion is conclusive; for is he not the composer of *Veni Creator*, guaranteed as excellent music by Professor Stanford and Dr Parry? You want to know who Dr Parry is? Why, the composer of *Blest Pair of Sirens*, as to the merits of which you have only to consult Dr Mackenzie and Professor Stanford.

Shaw was cynical of the artistic pretensions of audiences who went to concerts of sacred music to be uplifted. 'Dvorak's Requiem bored Birmingham so desperately that it was unanimously voted a work of extraordinary depth and impressiveness', and he was even more savage with Gounod's *Redemption*— 'I have no more to say generally than that if you will only take the precaution to go in long enough after it commences and to come

The interior of the Crystal Palace. A concert organised by the temperance movement. For the Handel Festivals, the audience would not be outnumbered by the choir, as is sadly in evidence here

out long enough before it is over you will not find it wearisome', and Brahms's Requiem was so dull that the flattest of funerals would be a ballet after it.

It would be too much to say that Shaw spelled quietus to the oratorio, for Elgar's *Dream of Gerontius* appeared long after Shaw had ceased to be a music critic. What is astounding is that no one of his calibre should have risen before to deflate the oratorio, to check the absurdities of its supporters ('the men who wrote the greatest Oratorios were the greatest Masters of Fugue that ever lived . . .').

Unquestionably the oratorio was a millstone round the neck of Victorian music, and although it was popular it was popular for the wrong reasons. That it was accepted as the supreme musical form in place of the symphony caused many composers to devote much time and energy in its propagation. Equally truly, the oratorio boom kept choirs in operation and singers and orchestral players at work. Many professional musicians looked upon oratorio as bread and butter music, and were correspondingly casual. At the London debut of *Elijah*, many players resented having to do anything more advanced than Handel, and showed it clearly to the composer. On the afternoon before the performance, Mendelssohn declared that he would not conduct. 'Oh, these tailors and shoemakers', he said, 'they cannot do it, and will not practice! I shall not go.' However, the promised presence of the Queen and Prince Albert spurred him to make the effort.

The standard of performance of oratorio was frequently deplorable. Soon after his election as a performing member of the Philharmonic Society the famous singer Charles Santley was called upon to take part in Haydn's oratorio *The Creation*, followed by *The Messiah*. A boy of fifteen, Santley was not disposed to be impressed by his fellow singers. 'Of those in my immediate vicinity', he wrote in his memoirs, 'I could not avoid remarking some to whom even a simple psalm-tune without accompaniment must have been a hard nut to crack.'

At another performance of this work under Hullah, the trumpet player was called away suddenly and as Santley was due

Although newer than the Three Choirs Festival, the festivals at Birmingham and Norwich were noted for their adventurous spirit. The Norwich Festival of 1866, *shown here, put on Costa's oratorio Naaman*

to sing 'The trumpet shall sound' this was extremely inconvenient. Hullah asked Santley if he would do it if the trumpet part was played on the organ, and Santley agreed. Santley was very adept at jumping into places vacated by solo singers who had either forgotten that they were to appear or had at the last moment found better employment than provincial oratorio. His ability to sight-read also placed him in demand for provincial festivals, such as Hereford and Worcester, when oratorios doomed to one performance only were promoted as if they were masterworks.

Nala and Damayanti (1871) by Ferdinand Hiller was one of these, 'of the numerous compositions of the same class which I had all the trouble of learning and rehearsing for a single performance'. Not that Santley was displeased; oratorio, though not in the same street as opera, was better than ballads ('imbecile trash about two old fogies warming their toes and indulging in sentimental balderdash').

The festivals were a great boon to home-grown oratorios. Besides the most famous, the triennial Three Choirs Festival (Worcester, Gloucester, and Hereford), there were the Sons of the Clergy Festival, the Norwich Festival, the important Birmingham Festival, instrumental in promoting Mendelssohn, and many cathedral festivals at Durham, Ely, Peterborough and Salisbury. In York in 1861 there was a festival in the Minster with 2,700 trained singers.

The Three Choirs Festival was started in 1724. Each festival was held in the various cathedrals in turn, and were strong in producing English oratorio. Originally they had been three-day events, but in 1836 they were made four day. Much to the embarrassment of the ecclesiastical authorities, the festivals made considerable profits—although the Three Choirs Festival at Gloucester in 1883 made only £500 clear and this was then a noteworthy feat.

The profit-making side of festivals was disagreeable to the devout and in 1875 an attempt was made at Worcester to banish oratorio, substituting church music and prayers, but this move signally failed. When Elgar, nurtured on the traditions of the Three Choirs Festivals, came to write his oratorio *Dream of Gerontius*, there was both a platform and an audience for it, if only for the obligatory single performance (fortunately for Elgar a series of performances of this work in Germany caused English critics to revise their opinion of one-shot oratorio).

Oratorio filled a need; it was the rice-pudding of music—starchy, filling, but rather uninteresting. It is to its credit that it gave employment to a good many worthy people at a time when composers had to get jobs as organists to survive, and it helped to keep alive the English choral tradition. It was by and large a harmless pursuit, like its contemporary, phrenology, and although it might have made the English music-lover more smug, encased in the belief that he or she was being made purer by being bored, oratorio may conceivably have opened the eyes of many to the more telling choral works of the past

The Three Choirs Festival of 1866 *was held at Worcester, and was criticised for making excessive profits and for the low standard of the performances*

CHAPTER TEN

THE TWO FACES OF OPERA

GRAND OPERA in the abstract hardly existed in Victorian London until the arrival of Wagner and the Wagner cult, and it tottered along for the edification of the upper classes, tolerated because it was the chosen vehicle for a small number of singers, whom not to have seen was social disgrace. These were four in number —Alboni, contralto, English debut 1847; Mario, tenor, English debut 1839; Grisi, soprano, English debut 1834; and Jenny Lind, soprano, English debut 1847, the Swedish nightingale, the only one of the four to establish herself in English folk lore.

All these performers were foreigners, and whereas it was all right for English singers to operate in drawing-room and oratorio, the native breed was considered too heavy and lumpish for opera. Opera, almost by definition, was Italian or German, or, reluctantly, French. English opera was all very well for provincials, and doubtless was useful as settings for popular ballads such as 'Home, Sweet Home', or 'I dreamt that I dwelt in marble halls', but it would really not do for the London opera house (literally— there was only His/Her Majesty's Theatre until 1847 when the Royal Italian Opera house (later, Covent Garden) opened as opposition).

The refusal to countenance English opera was a heritage from the eighteenth century, when Burney dominated musical think

A lavish production of Meyerbeer's opera L'Etoile du Nord at the Royal Italian Opera House in 1855. It is incredible that opera houses could afford to put on such spectacular shows with casts of hundreds, and elaborate sets

ing; Burney affirmed that the only good opera was Italian opera, and the nineteenth-century aristocracy turned this into dogma. It followed from this that only Italians could sing Italian opera as it was meant to be sung (and Jenny Lind was an Italian by proxy). It did not matter that Madame Alboni was fat and grotesque, or that Mario had the deportment of a gigolo or a dancing-master. 'He was the handsome, well-born romantic Italian tenor for whose coming society had so long been waiting', wrote Lord Ernest Hamilton, wondering why in the 1840s and 1850s opera-goers had prostrated themselves in the mud for him.

These four singers commuted between the various European capitals, with the Italian operatic composers writing works for them. Bellini wrote *Norma* and Rossini *Semiramide* for Grisi, and

no matter how shabbily the operas were presented, the adoration
for this quartet seemed endless, though some of the gilt rubbed
off when Mario married Grisi and thus robbed impressionable
young ladies of their heart's delight.

In retrospect it would seem that these singers would perform
anything to keep their name before the public. In her *Memories
of Ninety Years*, the artist Mrs E. M. Ward demonstrates this:

> Grisi and Mario I knew very well, and I shall never forget
> Grisi's rendering of 'The Minstrel Boy' at the Crystal
> Palace. She refused to sing again after three encores. The
> audience, who had listened to her singing spellbound, rose
> in a mass; the applause was like thunder. It seemed as if
> the glass roof would shatter, it was so tremendous.

But all pales into insignificance beside the adulation heaped
upon Jenny Lind. Jenny Lind was born in 1820, made her debut
in Stockholm, her native city, in Weber's *Freischutz* in 1838, and
had a trial in Paris, but as no engagement followed she vowed
never to play in Paris again. London therefore was one trick up
on Paris when Mlle Lind appeared in London, to the sound of
broken contracts and devious double-dealing, a ceremony of
hesitations and vacillations arranged by the theatrical promoters
to excite interest, culminating in the sad news that negotiations
had fallen through when, in fact, the engagement had been
signed and sealed. The PR work succeeded; London went mad
over Jenny Lind, tickets were sold and resold at astronomical
prices, and society ladies sat on the steps at the Opera, unable to
penetrate any further into the building.

Modest, becoming, a giver to charities (a point insisted upon
by the management), Jenny Lind was the ideal recipient of early
Victorian heroine-worship:

> Again were struggling crowds early at the door; again were
> hats doubled up and dresses torn; and again was the throng
> of carriages, the clamour and conflict of coachmen, servants,
> policemen, mob, the same as of yore.

The account is by Benjamin Lumley, the manager of the

Opera House, and the note of triumph is not difficult to hear, though this was to be muted, for two years after her debut in London, Jenny Lind retired from the operatic stage, went to America for a triumphant tour, married there the composer Otto Goldschmidt, and upon her return 'betook herself to the more congenial platform of the concert room'. Her pious appearance in her husband's oratorio *Ruth* did not have the drawing power of her 1847 appearances, though such engagements stamped 'her name in the Golden Book of singers'.

The operatic Jenny Lind of 1847 did not captivate all her audience. Present at a performance of *La Sonnambula*, Lady Charlotte Guest paid tribute to the voice and the manner in which she could hold a note till it died away imperceptibly, but thought she was a poor actress:

> Jenny Lind is painfully ugly, with a most unclassical profile, nez retroussé, light waving hair, small stature, low forehead, and inexpressive features.

Not unnaturally the opera-goers thought that they had been cheated by the premature disappearance of Jenny Lind, and were further displeased that she had made £20,000 in America and therefore did not have to sing in opera for a living; they did not believe that the whole of her American earnings was devoted to founding and endowing art scholarships in Sweden.

Still, there were the others, though Mario continued to act Mario in every operatic part he was given. However, *Don Giovanni* foxed him; the reckless profligate of the title role could not be reconciled with Mario's tepid romantic gent. In 1867 he left the stage, and died in some poverty in Rome. His wife, Grisi, left the stage in 1866, and died in 1869—when she was either fifty-seven, fifty-nine, or sixty-three (her birthdates vary). Alboni had retired nearly a decade before.

Although Madame Patti put in her appearances from 1861, and received the customary plaudits, opera-goers fervently wished for another Mario, and without a tenor Grand Opera went into a decline, though Wagnerian opera was in the ascendancy. In 1875, Carl Rosa started opera at the Princess's Theatre in

An opera audience of 1859, satirically observed

Oxford Street. In commissioning a British composer, Frederic Cowen, to write an opera, *The Lady of Lyons*, he made a cardinal error, for the prejudice against native talent had not softened over the years, but Rosa scored a signal success with Wagner, giving the first English performance of *The Flying Dutchman* at the Lyceum in 1876.

Unlike his theatrical predecessors, Carl Rosa did not scour the continent looking for singers that would appeal to the dress circle, but concentrated on good English singers carefully rehearsed and presented. He still thought there was a place for British opera, and once again the unfortunate Mr Cowen was the chopping-block, with his opera *Pauline*.

The devotees of Grand Opera, where the singer is all and aria succeeds to aria, scorned Wagner as being the antithesis of all that was good. No set pieces, no jettisoning of action to allow a quartet or a quintet, but only incomprehensible music and stage trickery that always threatened to get out of hand. But in Germany the obscure British composer Cipriani Potter, whose centenary has just passed without anyone being aware of it, noted something rather odd. The Reverend Haweis recalled a conversation he had had with Potter, 'when the English papers teemed with the usual twaddle about Wagner's music being intelligible only to the few'.

> It is all very well to talk this stuff here, but in Germany it is the people, the common people, who crowd to the theatre when *Tannhauser* and *Lohengrin* are given.

Haweis observed the same thing in the London opera houses. It was always the pit and the gallery who called for Wagner nights; a new adventurous audience for opera was growing in London, and in 1880 two of the London theatres gave their programmes over to Wagner, Covent Garden doing the whole of the *Ring* cycle of music dramas. The Wagner mania culminated in the hero-worship of Bernard Shaw, selling Wagner to yet another generation.

The fact that the Paris audience had whistled *Tannhauser* off the stage in 1861 spelled finis to Wagner so far as the traditional opera public was concerned. This public was still looking for a tenor successor to Mario. It found one in Jean de Reszké. Although de Reszké suffered from the initial disadvantages that he was neither Italian nor a tenor, the fashionable audience took him to their hearts, the boxes that had become almost derelict once more had the names of England's greatest and best on their doors, and the sovereigns once more rattled in Covent Garden.

De Reszké's success was partly due to the promotion of Lord and Lady de Grey, who at their house in Bruton Street entertained guests who were cajoled into doing their bidding. Lady de Grey, formerly Lady Gladys Herbert, then Countess of Lonsdale, sought amusement, whether it was bicycling during the cycling craze or aestheticism during the Oscar Wilde period. It would be agreeable, though she did not care overmuch for music, to revive the great age of Grand Opera. Not only did she promote de Reszké, but also Melba; de Reszké made his debut in 1887, Melba in 1888. Lady de Grey approved of the change of name from Nellie Armstrong—whatever opera was, it was not common.

The upsurge in Grand Opera was to some degree artificial, for Lady de Grey's interest in the subject was academic. In the words of that ironical observer of the scene, E. F. Benson, her aim was not to enjoy a first-rate operatic performance every night but to clean and wind up a shabby old clock and set it going and striking the hours. Whether she wanted it or not, the old days could not return, and there was an opera-going audience which was more interested in the new music than in catching the eye of Lady de Grey or basking in the approval of Society. There was also a management which had seen the success that Carl Rosa had had with Wagner, and de Reszké found himself singing Siegfried and Tristan rather than the Italian characters made memorable by Mario.

Every year from 1887 to 1900 de Reszké appeared in London, but Lady de Grey had new interests, and when he retired from the stage to breed race-horses in his native Poland and teach music in Paris in 1904, he was on the verge of outstaying his welcome. Lady de Grey took up the Russian ballet.

There are parallels between Victorian ballet, Grand Opera, and music hall. The executant was more important than the end product. It was an age of personalities. They were all popular in their various ways, for ballet and opera were brought to the

Late-Victorian operatic performers as they appeared to the unimpressed

Covent Garden Opera House. This is the 1858 building designed by Barry and built on the site of the earlier opera house opened for Italian opera in 1847

ordinary people via the music hall. It was fortunate that there were so many outlets for these art forms, and also that they could adapt to suit the changed conditions—ballet by merging with skirt-dancing, and opera by expanding, encompassing not only Wagner, but operetta, the musical comedy of the 'nineties, and that phenomenon that outsteps classification, Gilbert and Sullivan.

The breathing hot/breathing cold situation of opera in Britain did not help those who ardently wished for a national opera house in London. 1875 seemed a propitious year for building opera houses, and the first stone of the National Opera House was laid by the Duke of Edinburgh, the first brick having been laid by a celebrated singer of the time. The scheme was in ruins in 1877, the causes both physical and spiritual; the chosen site was on the Thames Embankment, that superb piece of Victorian town planning, but it was soon found that the foundations had been laid amidst springs and quicksands. Notwithstanding that an underground passageway connected with the Houses of Parliament and the District Railway, the project had to be abandoned, and in 1880 the building materials were sold. What had been built was pulled down in 1888, but the foundations remained, and were utilised by Norman Shaw in 1891 when New Scotland Yard was erected on the same site. The contrast of Pelleas and policemen cannot have appealed to the promoters of the National Opera House, for the scheme lost £100,000.

The other major essay in promoting the lost cause of an English opera house was in 1891, when D'Oyly Carte, made rich by Gilbert and Sullivan (D'Oyly Carte died worth a quarter of a million pounds) instructed the architect T. E. Collcutt to build a magnificent fire-proof, two thousand seat opera house in Cambridge Circus as homage to the serious Sullivan, divested of Gilbert. The Royal English Opera House opened with *Ivanhoe*, with a cast hired regardless of expense; after a hundred and fifty performances, *Ivanhoe* was withdrawn, and *La Basoche*, an obscure comic opera with music by Messager, replaced it, with occasional performances of *Ivanhoe* to show Sullivan that he was not forgotten. Almost exactly a year after it was opened the Royal English Opera House closed; when it reopened four and a half months later it was to Sarah Bernhardt, but no matter how she appealed to the late James Agate, the ticket-buying English public would have little of her, and her programmes lasted two months, whereupon the opera house was renamed the Palace Theatre of Varieties.

The building is still there, a sad monument to a laudable project. Once again, an opera by a British composer had failed lamentably, and Sullivan joins the catalogue of operatic composers who have had the thumbs down.

However, the knowledge that they were foredoomed never worried Victorian composers, and the corpses of their operas litter the years. Edward Loder with *Nourjahad* and *Francis I*, George Macfarren with *Charles II* and *Helvellyn*, William Wallace

Formerly the Royal English Opera House, the Palace Theatre was the most adventurous attempt to make English opera pay. Opening in 1888 with an opera by Sullivan, it was soon turned over to more mundane matters, managed by the most successful entrepreneur of the music hall, Charles Morton

with *Matilda of Hungary* and *The Desert Flower*, Julius Benedict's *The Brides of Venice*. Nor did it worry the promoters. Alfred Bunn (1796-1860) undertook in 1833 the joint management of Drury Lane and Covent Garden, in which he was vigorously opposed. Bunn's aim was the elevation of English opera; his only stipulation was that he should write the libretti.

Bumptious, quarrelsome, assaulted by the actor Macready, Bunn was the target of savage attacks by *Punch*, and when operas were produced at his theatres with his libretti, he was castigated as the Bardikin or the Poet Bunn. Unfortunately for *Punch*, he was the perfect provider of words for English opera, and his verses have a currency today of no mean order—he has two mentions in the concise Oxford *Dictionary of Quotations*, 'Alice, where art thou?' and 'I dreamt that I dwelt in marble halls'.

The latter song came from *The Bohemian Girl* (1843). It is difficult to be patronising about this opera by Balfe, words by Bunn, for not only was it a success in a field where successes were few and far between, but it is still, if only marginally, in the amateur repertory. It is replete with lines that catch the memory:

> When other lips and other hearts,
> Their tales of love shall tell;
> In language whose excess imparts
> The pow'r they feel so well.

If classical music is dominated by the three Bs—Bach, Beethoven, and Brahms—then so is early Victorian opera—Balfe, Bishop and Benedict, plus two more Bs for good measure to provide the words—Ball and Bunn. Balfe and Bishop were fluent composers, with a talent for grasping at a tune and setting it down without revision. Although their operas are a hotchpotch, their instinct for good melodies carried them through. Their lyrics were obtained by diving a hand into a metaphorical hat; this could pay dividends.

When Bishop came across 'Mid pleasures and palaces/Though we may roam/Be it ever so humble/There's no place like home', written by an obscure American actor, John Howard Payne, intuition told him that here was a gem. 'Home, Sweet Home' may be only a song from his opera *Clari: or the Maid of Milan*, but it epitomised a whole age. Without being particularly good composers, Balfe and Bishop, and on a slightly lower level, Benedict, had the key to the *zeitgeist*. Behind the door were the goodies that the Victorians were crying out for—custom-wrapped sentimentality and nostalgia.

The average Victorian was lazy in his musical tastes; the preference was for the familiar and not the new and demanding. He could be coaxed into listening to novelty, as he was by the conductor/impresario Jullien, but the pill had to be sugared. The members of the provincial choruses could be encouraged to sing in modern oratorio—if it went no further harmonically and intellectually than Mendelssohn. The music hall audience may appear to be an exception when confronted with ballets and operas, but they had no choice; they paid their shillings and they took their chances, and although they appreciated kinds of music with which they were not previously acquainted, to a large extent it was wished on them by enthusiasts for the golden age of the young queen. The kind of entertainment was immaterial; gaiety, atmosphere, food and drink, the escape from their own humdrum world, these were the factors that counted. When the audience did get a choice, when the growing music hall did a little grass roots research into consumer reaction, then it was found out what they really did want—rousing good ditties by the Lions Comique.

This hypothesis holds, too, with opera, though opera was far more diverse and complicated than ballet or oratorio. The upper classes ignored English opera, though they would go to hear their favourite singers doing songs from it. English opera was supported by the upper middles, especially the women. The sentiments were especially attuned to feminine feelings. The daughters of the house bought the popular numbers as sheet music and played them on the piano, or sang them to admiring friends of the same social class. It became natural to look upon English opera as a string of adorable airs linked in a way that was arbitrary or incomprehensible.

The fact that the songs came from opera gave them an extra *cachet*, for it proved that they were superior music. Musical snobbery reigned in middle-class homes, and the superficial sentiment of the songs was treated as if it was great thought made manifest. But why should sentiment be any more than superficial? By refusing to acknowledge the small moments of 1840, we are cutting ourselves off from the understanding of a social phenomenon.

The literary level of the English operatic song was that of the Christmas card:

> Scenes that are brightest
> May charm awhile

Hearts that are lightest
And eyes that smile;

Maritana 1845

The heart bow'd down by weight of woe
To weakest hopes will cling;
To thought and impulse while they flow,
That can no comfort bring,

The Bohemian Girl 1843

I'm but a simple peasant maid,
None e'er served or me obeyed,
My humble cot and woodland range
I would not for a palace change.

The Rose of Castille 1857

The response to simple song can be complex. Whether the above verses can be called curious is a matter of some doubt, but if this be allowed, an extract from Oscar Wilde's *The Critic as Artist* of 1891 may be relevant:

> I can fancy a man who had led a perfectly commonplace life, hearing by chance some curious piece of music, and suddenly discovering that his soul, without his being conscious of it, had passed through terrible experiences, and known fearful joys, or wild romantic loves, or great renunciations.

Did Balfe and Bishop, and their librettists, realise that they had tapped such a valuable vein? Balfe and Bishop certainly did. Their lyric writers were convinced anyway that they were possessed of genius and rapture over their products was no more than they deserved. Balfe was no simpleton wringing melodies out of his heart (like the popular idea of Schubert) but a proficient all-round musician with an eye for the main chance. Born in 1808, Balfe had his first violin lessons when he was five, and by the time he was seven he was able to score a piece of music. At ten he wrote a ballad that was afterwards sung by Madame Vestris

(1797-1856). When he was still in his teens he conducted a band at Drury Lane, and played the violin in oratorio. He was also an excellent singer, and sang in Italy until 1835, appearing at the Scala, Milan. He was in addition an impressario managing the Lyceum Theatre in 1840.

Enormously talented, it is a pity that the musical situation of the time encouraged him to take the easy option. There is an interesting description of him as a drawing-room lion:

> He found it a profitable business; his terms were high and he had a trick of disappearing as soon as he considered he had done enough for the money.

Of his 'When other lips', Hullah wrote: 'The town fairly went mad about it. Balfe's graceful but somewhat commonplace melody was exalted to the skies. The brows of Mr Bunn, the author of the words, might have ached under the laurels that were heaped upon them'.

The fluency of Balfe was amazing, and singers and writers knew that they could rely on him to provide music in almost as little time as it took them to tell him their needs. Balfe wrote 'Come into the garden, Maud' for the singer Sims Reeves, sending the opening bars to Reeves from Paris. 'This will do', wrote back Reeves, confident that he would have the song by return. The playwright and actor Dion Boucicault was, if anything, even more copious and spontaneous than Balfe, responsible for 140 original works and adaptations. He wanted a song for a play, and went to see Balfe, handing the words over to Mrs Balfe. Upon seeing the lyrics, Balfe composed the song immediately, but Mrs Balfe, knowing that there is a limit to professionalism, sent Boucicault away, telling him to call back the following day.

Henry Bishop did not have the range of Balfe's abilities, but he was equally prolific, writing operas, ballets, adapting European operas with misplaced bravura, and trying his hand at sacred music, at which, as Grove's *Dictionary of Music and Musicians* would put it, he was a villa builder trying to erect a cathedral. *The Seventh Day* (1833) may have helped him capture a degree as Bachelor of Music at Oxford in 1839, for it showed the musical establishment that Bishop's heart was in the right place.

As composer and director of music at Covent Garden Theatre, Bishop was in the perfect position to promote his own music, and in 1830 he was appointed musical director at Vauxhall Gardens. A generation older than Balfe, Bishop's complete works are altogether forgotten, and the drawing-room songs filleted from his operas are out of currency, except for 'Home, Sweet Home'.

This was a song for bringing the house down, sung as an encore by Jenny Lind, the song Patti selected to sing when she was discovered sitting on a sofa in the Arundel Hotel, Norfolk Street. At a charity concert at the Albert Hall, a lady in the audience was so overcome that she immediately handed over a cheque for £1,000. Even Queen Victoria was not immune, and her donation was more startling still—a knighthood in 1842, whereupon Bishop turned his face on opera and churned out works the fate of which were one performance or, as in the case of an oratorio, *The Fallen Angel*, no performance at all. The oratorio-loving public did have some standards.

Although William Wallace (1814-65) enjoyed with his opera *Maritana* (1845) a success equal to that of *The Bohemian Girl*, although tunes from *Maritana* found their way into the drawing room—such as 'Angels that around us hover'—he did not have the grasping, rapacious dispositions of Balfe or Bishop. He did not stay in the purlieus of Covent Garden where reputations were made, and did not wheedle his way into the confidence of the theatrical promoters.

He was born in Ireland of Scottish parentage, leaving Dublin in his early twenties to seek fame and fortune in Australia, moving from there to South and North America, writing music and performing en route. A concert in Peru netted him £1,000. 1845 found him in a private box in London, dressed as a cotton planter, and a friend asked him if he thought that he could write an opera. 'Certainly', replied Wallace, 'twenty', and he was immediately provided with the book of *Maritana*, written by Bunn and Ball. By this time Ball was flush with success and had renamed himself Fitzball.

Bunn followed that libretto with an appallingly bad one for *Matilda of Hungary*, and disappointed by the reaction of the public, Wallace went to Germany where he stayed fourteen years, writing agreeable piano music in a diluted Chopinesque manner. Although he made visits to Britain and composed another opera that had popular success—*Lurline* (1860)—Wallace never received the plaudits and honours of Balfe and Bishop, though he was a better composer and enjoyed the respect of perhaps the most able composer of the day, Sterndale Bennett.

Julius Benedict was a one opera man so far as the opera-loving public was concerned—*The Lily of Killarney* (1862), though single numbers were dredged from his earlier operas for drawing-room consumption. 'Rage thou angry storm', from *The Gypsy's Warning* was once a favourite bass aria for home circles. Like Wallace, Benedict narrowly escaped being a composer of the first rank, and was a key figure in Victorian high music, conducting at every Norwich Festival from 1845 to 1878, involved in the presentation of classical concerts in London, writing a book on Weber, and composing a symphony besides the obligatory oratorio. His knighthood was better deserved than Bishop's.

Balfe, Bishop, Wallace and Benedict could afford to write operas. Their musical activities were widespread, either in organisation or in different fields of composition. The income from the songs taken from the operas was considerable, and unlike the composers of songs for music hall and song and supper room they drove hard bargains. An air written in a day was worth hundreds and sometimes thousands of pounds.

Their worldly success forms a strange accompaniment to the always insecure place of English opera on the stage, and it must be remembered that there were dozens of composers whose names are completely forgotten endeavouring to write an operatic hit, composers without an entrée into the fashionable circles of Covent Garden, composers who were misled by the adulation that *The Bohemian Girl* had received into believing that opera was in a healthy state. It was the fate of opera theatres to either burn down or to come to grief on English opera.

CHAPTER ELEVEN

BALLET

THE MOTIVATIONS OF the ballet-lover of the Victorian age were mixed. The cult of the performer, the pleasure in seeing scantily clad young ladies on the stage, these vied with the appeal of the music. Those who were ready to be appalled by the immodesty of dress took assurance from Queen Victoria, who placed the seal of respectability on ballet and ballet-dancers by visiting a ballet in 1843.

Nevertheless, ballet was never entirely accepted by the landed gentry, and there is a significant entry in Lady Frederick Cavendish's diary, dated 28 May 1859:

> We've been to the Opera! *Gazza Ladra* at Covent Garden, Lord Ward's box. There being no ballet, Papa let us go.

One name dominates Victorian ballet, Marie Taglioni. She arrived in England in 1829 and for the next twenty years ballet held a place in London that it was never to hold again. She had put Paris in thrall in 1827, Auber writing a ballet for her, and she did the same thing in London, her 'virginal and diaphanous art foreshadowing undreamt-of possibilities'. Although Rossini was held to be advanced, Taglioni did not debase her programmes to suit the English ignorance. *William Tell* was smuggled into the ballet repertoire as *The Tyrolienne*, danced in 1830, followed in

Taglioni was the best known of the ballet stars, a legend in her own lifetime

1832 by *La Sylphide*, for which Taglioni received £100 a night and was guaranteed two benefits totalling £1,000. Her father received £600 for acting as ballet master, and her brother and sister-in-law were employed on stage to assist her at a salary of £900.

This was at a time when serious music in England was tottering along on a shoe-string, when there were only two societies to carry on the English tradition of choral music, when the programmes of the one organisation promoting classical music on anything like a tolerable scale, the Ancient Concerts, were 'slovenly performed and carelessly conducted' through lack of money. Musical appreciation in the London of the 1830s was decidedly lop-sided.

Taglioni—never prefixed by Miss or Mlle—married the Comte Gilbert des Voisins in 1832, to whom she bore a son, but this did not detract from her popularity, though it is interesting that she soon parted from him to devote her life to her art. She gave her name to a type of coach and a great coat, and Thackeray was full of praise for her. In 1831 another dancer came to London to challenge her supremacy—two dancers, in fact, the Elssler sisters, but Taglioni was in full command of the scene, and in 1834 the Elsslers were bribed away from London to Paris.

It was well known that the *corps de ballet* were fair game to men about town on the make, and the Elssler sisters soon gave indications that they, too, were obtainable. Fanny Elssler won the heart of the puny son of Napoleon, and became the mistress of the historian Grote. Her sister Thérése married Prince Adalbert of Prussia, and became Baroness Barnim. Royalties were apt to marry ballerinas. In 1892, Duke Ludwig of Bavaria married a Munich dancer forty years his junior; in 1847, the mad King Ludwig, Wagner's patron, contracted an alliance with a Miss Gilbert, who had appeared in London in 1843 as 'Lola Montez the Spanish Dancer'. Miss Gilbert exchanged this title for Baronne de Rosenthal and Comtesse de Lansfeldt.

The ballet was known as 'the hot-bed of seduction' and the young ladies of the corps de ballet were regarded as fair game by the young men about town. From a print of 1845

It is therefore understandable that there was always an eager supply of recruits to the *corps de ballet*. Working under atrocious conditions and for minimal wages, these poor undernourished girls dreamed of climbing into the nobility. Unfortunately they had neither the beauty, presence nor ability of Taglioni.

The Elssler sisters blossomed in the rapture of their Parisian welcome, and when Fanny visited America in 1839 she made 179 appearances and netted £39,000. Fanny was perhaps more versatile than Taglioni, and was adept in national dance; Spanish dances were enjoying a vogue. When she returned to England to dance before the Queen, the rivalry between her and Taglioni knew no bounds, each trying to top the other in stage gymnastics. The matter was not improved when a new rival appeared in 1840, Francesca Cerito. Cerito had the ear of the conductor at the

More versatile than her great rival Taglioni, Fanny Elssler made a speciality of Spanish dance, as shown here

*Grisi was one of the
stars of the ballet mania
of the 1840s*

Opera House, Michael Costa, a flashy conductor/composer who
was said to be able to get through all Beethoven's nine symphonies in an evening and still leave time for supper. In 1842
Costa composed a ballet, *Alma*, for Cerito.

There were further challenges in store for Taglioni and Fanny
Elssler, who had now eclipsed her sister. In 1842, Carlotta Grisi
appeared in *Giselle*, a ballet written for her by Gautier and
Adolphe Adam. *Giselle* is still in the repertoire, a somewhat
macabre tale of *wilis*—maidens who have died before their
wedding day and who come out of their graves at night in bridal
dress to dance until dawn. Woe betide any man who comes across
the *wilis* at work. The music by Adam was written in a week,
and it sounds like it.

No doubt Taglioni and Elssler would have been glad for Grisi to join the ranks of the *wilis* at the first convenient opportunity, for not only was Grisi's husband arranging ballets for Costa and was therefore disconcertingly near the seat of power, but she was much younger. Taglioni and Elssler were well into their thirties, Grisi was not yet out of her teens. Short on technical accomplishment, she had as compensation a complexion 'like a briar rose, a shy, sparkling pair of eyes, and a certain modest grace'.

In 1844 she captivated London with her performance in a ballet called *La Perie*, and it would seem that she would rise above all her predecessors as the prima ballerina of the 1840s. The manager of the theatre recruited a composer of ballet music, Pugni, to write music for Grisi. The result was a ballet based on Hugo's *The Hunchback of Notre Dame*. So great was the theatre manager's enthusiasm that he applied to the German poet Heine for the makings of a ballet, and Heine obliged with a scenario based on the Faust legend, in which Grisi was to appear as a female Mephistopheles. It was completely unsuitable for production, and the manager, Benjamin Lumley, returned to his hacks, who at least knew their business.

To European ballet dancers London was the Mecca of the 1840s, and in 1845 Lucille Grahn entered the arena to start a season under Lumley. This time Lumley, striving manfully under a *folie de grandeur*, overplayed his hand. Cerito and Grahn started the season with him, but Grisi and Taglioni were contracted to appear. How was he to appease them? He solved the problem by arranging a *Pas-de-Quatre* in which each of the four dancers would do her particular speciality, combining with the others for a grand climax. Grisi's husband was deputised to arrange all this, but on the day of production he found that none of the ladies would agree on precedence. Fortunately Lumley was by profession a lawyer. 'Let the oldest lady take her unquestionable right to the envied position', he said, an offer that was quadrilaterally declined.

With this *Pas-de-Quatre*, early Victorian ballet reached its apex. 'From the palace to the shop-counter', declared Lumley, 'the *Pas de Quatre* was the great topic of the day, to the exclusion

Taglioni.   Cerito.   Grahn.
              Grisi.

According to most historians of ballet, the pas de quatre performed by the principal ballet dancers of 1845 was the most important event in the history of the genre. It owed its inception to the fact that the management had booked too many of the top names
of every interest, however serious. The excitement crossed the Channel. Foreign papers circulated histories and descriptions of its wonders. Foreign Courts received, along with official despatches detailed accounts of its extraordinary captivations'.

Grove's *Dictionary of Music and Musicians* describes this dance, formulated to avoid costly tantrums, as 'one of the greatest triumphs of Terpsichorean Art on record'.

Sixteen years had now passed since Taglioni had first performed in London, and although she lived until 1884 there was no way for her after this coup except down. Fanny Elssler retired from the stage in 1851. Other dancers came and went, such as Madame Guy Stephan (fl. 1841-54) and Louise Fleury, but at no time was there the competition between great stars that had brought in the massive audiences for ballet.

This was not the first time that the cult of personality promoted a revival of an art form that was at odds with its environment, resulting in good music and work for musicians, and one wonders whether ballet would have survived without Taglioni and her contemporaries. Certainly Taglioni was a name known to all, even those who had never been to a ballet in their life, and in the 1870s she is referred to in music hall song ('She dances like Taglioni'). Of course there were other factors that made ballet a going concern in early Victorian England; it fitted in well with the romantic revival in its innocence and purity. The first shadows of the Industrial Revolution were making nostalgia for the rural past fashionable, simplicity was a quality that was increasingly lacking in the accelerating tempo of modern life, and ballet mirrored the mood, being useless, pretty, and utterly remote from life.

The replacement of the gross band of Georges by the sweet virtuous Victoria was also a factor that played its part in the interest in ballet. There was also the belief that the new age would be one of delicacy and artistic endeavour, that somehow the machine era would be cloaked and draped with the elegaic equippage of the past. Eventually it was seen that this was not to be, and a more self-conscious look into the past produced the Gothic Revival.

The upsurge of ballet in these twenty early Victorian years left an indelible mark on the history of ballet. The dress of classical ballet of today is the dress of the 1830s, and although there was only one major technical development, the use of the tips of the toes, les pointes, to many people this one feature epitomises ballet—artificial, remote, and slightly ridiculous. The adoration heaped upon the ballerinas of the time is echoed by modern writers. Arnold Haskell in his book Ballet (1938) is no whit less enthusiastic than the fashionable theatre-goer of a hundred years previously:

Cerrito floats over a waterfall, Taglioni walks among the tree-trops to gather a nest, moves across a meadow without disturbing a blade of grass. There are wings to suggest movement, never muscles.

Notwithstanding their somewhat suspect private lives, the ballerinas were refined in the awful sense of the word. Taglioni has been called the first Christian dancer; her art was devoid of sex appeal. The cynical described her as being a dancer for women.

The dichotomy between the never-never land of the ballet and the grubby world outside, the prancing ranks of the ballet girls providing a background for the exertions of the key dancers, inviolate in their white muslin, all too vulnerable in the back streets of Drury Lane, led to the sudden decline of ballet in the theatres. Ballet became a handmaiden to opera.

This primitive use of the star system might well have been the undoing of early Victorian ballet; by demanding astronomical fees, the ballerinas priced themselves and their art out of the market. Furthermore, they were appealing to a fickle audience, theatre-goers who were more interested in saying that they had seen Taglioni dance than in going again to see her.

It is difficult to say what induced the new music hall to take ballet from its lofty pedestal in the Patent Theatres and plant it on the stages of the masses. There was certainly a demand for culture for all, and to gratify it the founder of music hall, Charles Morton, added an art gallery annexe to his Canterbury Music Hall and staged opera. His motto was 'One quality only— the best'.

However it was not the Canterbury Music Hall that was most assiduous in the presentation of ballet, nor the Metropolitan of South London, both of which maintained large ballet companies, but the Alhambra, which enjoyed a supremacy in this field until challenged by the Empire in 1887. Most of the ballets put on by the Alhambra were eminently forgettable, but it did promote works such as *Die Fledermaus*, Offenbach's *Orpheus in the Underworld*, and Auber's *The Bronze Horse*, and in doing so made the tunes from these memorable. Such tunes formed a standard repertoire for brass bands, military bands, and municipal orchestras such as the Bournemouth Municipal Orchestra, whose first concert given on 22 May 1893 is for the most part made up of music made familiar by exposure in the music halls:

March	The Standard Bearer	Fahrbach
Overture	Raymond	Thomas
Valse	Je t'aime	Waldteufel
Ballet Music	Rosamonde	Schubert
Mazurka	La Czarine	Ganne
Entracte	La Colombe	Gounod
Selection	The Gondoliers	Sullivan

Good music owes a debt to the music hall that it can never repay, and it was an error of judgment for serious composers such as Parry to sneer at the music hall as the home of everything that was cheap and vulgar. In its encouragement and propagation of music of consequence, the music halls did considerably better than those whose business it was to refute the German maxim that England was a land without music.

No dancers of the stature of Taglioni or Elssler rose during the period when the music hall was busy promoting ballet, and it was for a dancer trained at the Grecian Saloon to point the way to the future. This was Kate Vaughan, the first person to make 'skirt-dancing' popular. In skirt-dancing the steps are of little importance; it was the effect that mattered. Miss Vaughan's skirt-dancing led to a 'mere exhibition of whirling draperies under many-coloured lime-lights', eventually to forms of dancing in which the choreographer was of more significance than the dancer, demonstrated at its most lavish in the musical films of the 1930s.

Kate Vaughan represented a dance form midway between true ballet and the extrovert dancing of the late Victorian stage—the cancan, the splits, the cellar flap dance. It hinted more than it showed, and although muscular calves and thighs were hidden beneath petticoat and skirt, It had more sensual appeal than ballet. Kate Vaughan also made something of a fetish of long black gloves.

In first appearing at the Gaiety Theatre in 1872, Miss Vaughan managed to entice away many of the Alhambra patrons, and although she left the Gaiety to become a serious actress, she returned to dancing, commanding £70 a week. She never received the honour of being referred to by her surname only; she was always Miss Vaughan, never Vaughan.

It may be that Taglioni and her rivals were a unique group of dancers who happened to appear at precisely the right historical moment, and whatever their merits as dancers they did succeed in staving off for two decades the encroaching sea of Victorian vulgarity.

CHAPTER TWELVE

THE DANCING YEARS

THE PASSION FOR dancing in the nineteenth century cut across all social levels, and up to about 1860 a wide variety of new dances were introduced into the country, to be taken up or speedily dropped. Without exception, these dances were of the type now known today as Old Time Dances, and even in the casinos and dancing saloons of the lowest order, couples were engaged in the unpassionate and hectic figures of quadrilles and polkas. The only difference was that in the casinos the men kept their hats on, whereas at balls and county dances they took them off.

Between 1860 and the end of the century only two new dances were introduced into the repertory, and one of these, the Washington Post of 1894, was a short-lived novelty, though the other, the Barn Dance of 1888, remains with us. The only marginal exception was the Cake Walk, taken up in the industrial provinces towards the end of the century.

That dancing matters had remained stagnant from the death of the Prince Consort is evident from the following extract from *Manners and Tone of Good Society* by 'a Member of the Aristocracy' (c 1895):

> The *only* dances danced by 'society' are 'quadrilles', 'lancers', 'valses', 'the Highland Scottische', 'the Highland reel', and the 'polka', which has taken the place so long occupied by the galop. Country dances, such as the

'Tempete', 'Sir Roger de Coverley', &c., are usually danced at private balls when given in the country; and often a London ball concludes with a 'cotillion', in which expensive presents are sometimes given. Such dances as the 'Caledonians', the 'Mazurka', 'Prince Imperial quadrilles', &c., are unknown in good society.

The three dances stigmatised by the writer were not necessarily more risky or suggestive than the others. They had merely been refused admittance to the canon by some arbitrary quirk of class. The impression that this gives of the aristocracy scampering endlessly across acres of ballroom floor, with an occasional breather in the form of a waltz, is not denied by the facts. The waltz, again, was of the Old Time variety, rapid and devoid of the sensual connotations of modern ballroom dancing.

When Victoria came to the throne in 1837, the waltz was in the process of being accepted by society. In 1829, Mr G. Yates, a dancing master, had defended it as 'one of the most graceful of dances when well danced to a gentle measure'. It had been more or less respectable since about 1812, when it was introduced at the exclusive Almack's Assembly Rooms, King Street, St James's, and it was welcomed because it was a 'closed' dance, that is, there were no changes of partner. It was therefore the first modern dance, in which dance as a social phenomenon is given precedence to dance as a means of communicating with a member of the opposite sex.

Queen Victoria was fond of dancing. She was, after all, a high-spirited girl in her late teens with all the appetites of her Hanoverian ancestry. With her 'slim figure and fine bust' (as a reporter of *The Town* saw her) she looked well on the dance floor. She was the last person to cut herself off from innocent pleasures because of protocol, because there was still a body of opinion that considered the waltz indecent.

In 1840 the polka made its appearance in Paris, but it was not until 1843 that it seized the public imagination. The *Times* correspondent in Paris reported: 'Politics is for the moment suspended in public regard by the new and all-absorbing pursuit, the Polka'. In 1844, the polka came to London, danced first of all on the stage of Her Majesty's Theatre by two celebrated ballet dancers of the period. Like the waltz, the polka was a closed dance, and evidence of its popularity was soon apparent. At a ball given by the aged Duke of Wellington at Apsley House in honour of Queen Victoria's birthday, the polka was danced six times during the course of the evening. This, to the savants, broke into the established pattern of ballroom dancing (quadrille, waltz, quadrille, polka or other dance, quadrille, waltz, quadrille, polka or other dance).

The craze for the imported dance was known as polkamania, but even without the polka the sudden enthusiasm for dancing would not have been quelled. In 1845 the *Thé Dansant* was introduced; this 5 o'clock Tea Dance was described by *Punch* as 'the nearest approach to which seems to have been the capers cut by a bull among the cups and saucers in a china-shop'. The appeal of the polka was so widespread that it was simplified for greater assimilation, and in this later form it remained popular throughout the century. George Grossmith's 1886 song 'See Me Dance the Polka' is a reminder of this.

Although the waltz and the polka were challengers to the quadrille, introduced to dancing circles in 1815, the old style of dancing received a fillip from the general revival of dancing. In 1817 the lancers, a variant of the quadrille, was born, but it was not danced in respectable circles until 1850, when it was promoted by Madame Sacré, a dancing teacher of Hanover Square. She did this by persuading four of her former pupils to dance the lancers at the fashionable balls in the Season. Highly placed in society, these girls succeeded in winning a permanent place for the lancers in ballroom programmes.

Originally the lancers was a specific tune, 'The Lancers', but it became so popular that it was clear that other tunes would have to be found for it. Lecocq's opera *La Fille de Madame Angot* (1872) was plundered for likely lancer material, and this was the fate also of Sullivan's *Trial by Jury* and Sidney Jones's *The Geisha*. The lancers eclipsed the quadrille except at Court Balls and Assemblies.

The mazurka was the ballroom dance introduced in the 1840s in opposition to the polka

Seeing the amazing effect that the polka had had, there were several attempts to introduce other European modes of dance, such as the mazurka and the polonaise. The mazurka did not catch on, so the promoters invented the hybrid, the polka-mazurka, which similarly died a slow death. The marriage between Victoria and Prince Albert had made the import of foreign products respectable, and although it was not a German dance, Prince Albert led the Queen in a polonaise to open a Costume Ball at Buckingham Palace in 1846.

The cotillon received a measure of support at fashionable balls, especially at the end of the evening when aristocratic feet and ankles were tired. It was a grown-up version of musical chairs. In 1863 a cotillon begun at two in the morning went on until five. Cotillons also had an auxiliary function; it was customary to present the ladies with flowers, but as time went by flowers were not deemed enough, and hostesses bribed hesitant guests to come to their balls by offering magnificent presents (at a lower level, flags of all the nations were offered by firms to cotillon addicts for a few pence a set).

Another dance that was admitted to fashionable balls was the schottische. The titled had more difficulty in spelling it (qv the

State balls could be occasions of chill formality, and in this engraving of 1863 it would be difficult to discern that the grand personages were dancing the quadrille

anonymous Member of the Aristocracy) than dancing it, for it was a fairly brainless round dance, and had its come-uppance in Warne's *Ballroom Guide* (c 1860), which denounced it as 'irretrievably vulgar'.

A typical State Ball of the 1840s would open with a set of quadrilles, followed by waltzes. There would be a break while the Queen rested, the band playing a quadrille or two as background music, then there would be more quadrilles, waltzes, and a couple of polkas until supper was taken at midnight. After supper the guests had to endure or enjoy a session of bagpipe music, before another group of quadrilles and waltzes. The Ball would end about two.

This pattern was kept up throughout the century, the Prince of Wales continuing the tradition when the Queen was too old. Occasionally the lancers were used instead of a quadrille set. Country dances were decidedly out, though they lingered on in Hunt Balls.

After the death of the Prince Consort, the dancing enthusiasm died a little in deference to the Queen's decades of mourning, and unquestionably this decline of popularity was greeted warmly by many of the Top Ten Thousand, who had been obliged by fashion to attend so many balls and dances. The aristocracy were notoriously bad dancers, especially the men. Those who really liked dancing were content with what were known as home balls. In her diary, 6 June 1859, Lady Frederick Cavendish described a home ball:

> A little past two, after *the* pleasantest home ball, that's to say dance, for it was carefully distinguished from a ball by its smallness, absence of champagne, and substitution of modest pianoforte and harp for band.

Those members of the upper classes living on a tight budget were glad that the giving of great balls was no longer required of them. It could be an expensive business. Typical of the grand ball was one given by the Marchioness of Salisbury at Hatfield House in 1895. There were seven hundred guests, and two large bands. The women were expected to use the occasions as a means of conspicuous display, carrying a large bouquet of violets when violets were out of season and thus extremely expensive.

The etiquette of the fashionable ball could also be tricky. A hostess giving a ball in London who provided programmes was speedily downgraded in the eyes of her guests; programmes were all right for country balls. A hostess who expected guests to bring their invitation cards with them was likewise in trouble; guests would only do this for a masked ball. The word 'ball' was never used on the invitation card. An ordinary 'At Home' card was used, with 'Dancing' printed in the corner. Heaven help the husband who initiated invitations, for this was the pre-rogative of the wife.

The State Balls at Buckingham Palace demonstrate clearly that they were occasions for social one-upmanship rather than pleasure. The ladies wore full evening dress, the men either uniform or full court dress—dress coat, breeches and silk stockings and buckles. If the uniformed guest happened to go with his sword, then he would be etiquette-bound to wear it throughout the evening.

A key figure in Victorian fashionable dancing was the dancing master or mistress. These were figures of fun in Restoration England, when they were usually French or Italian with comical

Entry into the right circles was effected by good dancing, and although dancing masters were figures of fun they did wield considerable influence

accents, but in the nineteenth century they had to be taken more seriously, though perhaps not so seriously as they took themselves, ennumerating the various figures of the quadrille and waltz with a gravity that was, to say the least of it, sadly misplaced. Their jargon exemplifies their conceit. There was Mr Tenniel of Gloucester Place, London, who announced to the 'nobility, gentry, and his friends, that his course of instruction included Dancing, Deportment and modified Calisthenics, with his Systolic and Dyastolic Staff'.

At State Balls the dancing master was a privileged outsider, there to organise discreetly the frequently complex manoeuvres that made up open dancing. Lady Frederick Cavendish gives an account of a State Ball that did not have the cold formality that one is led to expect. The date is 1 May 1855:

> The Queen and the Royalties went to a sort of low platform at one end; and a fat duchess stood on each side of the Queen and Prince. Then the dance began, the Royalties dancing with the rest. But the whole was a sort of romp, the little ones not knowing exactly what to do, and an unfortunate dancing master in vain endeavouring to establish order.

It was the aim of conscientious parents not to have children who would create a shambles out of a grand occasion. If their progeny could not dance well, at least a dancing master could teach them not to trip over a Royal.

Men of mature years did not scorn the dancing master. A. G. C. Liddell was a sporting lawyer and man about town. In 1870, when he was twenty-four, Liddell came to London to start work at the Bar:

> In this pursuit I found myself considerably handicapped by my want of skill in dancing. It was therefore arranged that I should attend at M. D'Egville's house in Conduit Street and have some private lessons. This was a very trying performance. I was turned into a room with two active young women, who in turn played the piano and whirled me round on a stretched crumb-cloth.

Dancing academies proliferated during the 1850s and 1860s simply because boy could meet girl without too much interference from the chaperons

At times, for deserving charities and so forth, the upper classes forced themselves to attend public dances, but the social differences were as pronounced here as they were in the world outside; a section of the ballroom was roped off for them, so that they would not be forced to mingle with the middle and professional classes.

The dancing saloons of the West End were frequented, despite their reputations as haunts of sin and folly, by a wide variety of men and women. Some of the more respectable were run by dancing masters and mistresses, whose pupils, mainly girls, would bring their friends, male and female, at so much a head, refreshments and supper included. These girls belonged to the lower middle class, well-to-do shop girls, and paralleled the *grisette* class of Paris

Other dancing places deserved their reputation. Situated in or near the Haymarket, the centre of night life in the mid-Victorian period, were the Argyll Rooms, the dancing saloon of the celebrated Kate Hamilton (swathed in jewellery and wobbling like a blancmange when she laughed), 'The Pic', on the site of the present Criterion Theatre, where smashed hats and bloody noses were commonplace, and a number of other places including the night houses, a peculiar Victorian institution which was a cross between a night-club and a rendezvous for prostitutes.

The Argyll Rooms were not the Argyll Rooms of the eighteenth century. Although it catered for the smartest men about town and the cream of the London courtesans, it was not expensive, half a crown being the charge for admission. In between dances the ladies could partake of such favoured drinks of the period as brandy and soda or sherry and seltzer at one and sixpence a glass; champagne was twelve shillings a bottle.

Men of tone did not dance there except on Saturdays, and when they went in the week it was either as somewhere to go after the music halls and theatres had closed or to pick up a girl. To preserve the image of the Argyll (or 'The Duke's' as it was generally known) as a dancing saloon, capable dancers of both sexes were admitted free. Every evening a police inspector and sergeant would pay a visit to see that the place was not being kept as a disorderly house, but this supervision was not sufficient, for in 1878 the Middlesex magistrates yielded to puritan clamour and refused the Argyll a licence. It became a restaurant for four years, but this failed, and the property was bought to be turned into a music hall, the Trocadero.

Willis's, also known as Frere's, was situated near Langham Church, and was considered a good deal more respectable than the Argyll, just as the Holborn Saloon was considered just that little more raffish than the Argyll. Willis's catered for ladies of the aristocracy who wished for a minimum of discreet fun. Run by a Mr Frere, this saloon held two dances a week, and was frequented by military men and professional people plus a sprinkling of university undergraduates. Although Mr Frere was undermining the strict rules of class by permitting the upper classes to flirt with their inferiors, it is evident that Willis's filled a long-felt want, and it is an instance of how easy it was to break away from the shackles of class.

The Argyll was closed down by withdrawing its licence. Many of the saloons and night houses had no licences to withdraw. The Piccadilly Saloon, 'The Pic', was one of these. Situated in the Haymarket opposite to where the London Pavilion now stands, 'The Pic' was kept open by the simple expedient of bribing the local police, in particular an Inspector Silverton. Fun began at the Piccadilly Saloon at 12.30 am, and continued to the early hours. The place should have been visited every night by the police to ascertain that there was no drinking or dancing, but on the rare occasions when they did call it was customary for the officer to knock on the outer door, allow two or three minutes to transpire while the message was circulated, and then enter, by which time the three-piece band (pianist, harpist and violinist) would have disappeared and the drink would have been replaced by cups of coffee. Knowing that the three musicians were hiding in a large cupboard that led off the dance room, the inspector and his two subordinates would walk round, and go off again. Inspector Silverton controlled the entire area, and establishments of the same kind were kept open by his turning a blind eye. He was eventually forced to retire by the Marlborough Street magistrate, to live on the small fortune he had accumulated by accepting bribes.

The dancing saloons were living on the edge of the law, and attendance at these therefore carried with it an extra element of excitement. Men who would shun being picked up by a prostitute in the Haymarket would welcome the ambiguity of the dancing saloon, where the time-honoured approach of the girl was 'May I have the pleasure of paying my addresses to you, sir?'

The ironical thing was that these girls could dance. Ballet was known as 'the hot bed of seduction' and many fallen girls had graduated from the opera theatres to the dancing saloons, acting as hostesses and even dance instructors.

Between the dancing saloons and the fashionable ballrooms of the great country houses were the Assemblies. Assemblies were 'conducted' rather than 'run', and among the most popular was an Assembly held three times a week during the Season by Edward Humphrey at the Cavendish Rooms in Mortimer Street. The conductors of Assemblies frequently had interests in other forms of entertainment or had a financial concern in dancing—Humphrey's father was the inventor of a number of modish dances, and he himself started in 1892 the *Dancing Times*. Mr Piaggo conducted an Assembly in Winsley Street, Oxford Circus, hiring on special occasions the Portman Rooms in Baker Street. He owned the Marine Palace at Margate. Holborn Town Hall was also hired for Assemblies, as was the Kilburn Athenaeum. Assemblies were big business, sometimes catering for 2,000 people, and their organization and ethos is the nearest parallel the Victorians had to modern ballroom dancing—classless, sober and restrained.

This cannot be said of the open air dancing carried out in the pleasure gardens of Vauxhall and Cremorne. The pressures of the middle classes eventually closed these down, as they did the dancing saloons of the Haymarket, but at their peak there was a wealth of entertainment to be found in the London pleasure gardens, from freak shows to classical concerts.

A graphic description of the dancing at Cremorne was given by Francis Wey, a Frenchman who visited London in the 1850s:

> In a Chinese bandstand an orchestra struck up a schottische. A minute later the carefully levelled open space was filled with couples and the surrounding tables with onlookers. We took our seats and the waiter uncorked a couple of oval-shaped bottles and poured us out a frothy sparkling liquid which might have been lemonade had it not tasted of pepper and pimentos. This fashionable refreshment sets the roof of your mouth on fire, and while I still gasped for breath, Lionel (Wey's mentor through London low life) seized the hand of a young person of doubtful morality and flung himself with entire abandon into a Bacchanalian rendering of the polka. People dance here with their hips and their shoulders, seeming to have little control over their

legs. They have no ear for time. Frivolous young things improvise all sorts of indecorous antics.

This passage from a virtually unknown book is worth quoting at length because it demonstrates how the restrained dances of the ballroom could be turned into a libidinous riot by a change of attitude. The polka and waltz situations were amended by the environment. This could also be an unconscious operation; in answer to the unspoken demand for a dance that was passably erotic, the waltz gradually slowed down in the 1890s, though it still remained far more lively than the present ballroom waltz.

CHAPTER THIRTEEN

OUTDOOR MUSIC

VICTORIAN LONDON WAS alive with the sound of music. 'In retired streets, squares, terraces, or rows, where the more pleasing music of cart, coach, and cab wheels does not abound, the void is discordantly filled up by peripatetic concerts, which last all day long'. The complainant was Charles Dickens' weekly journal *Household Words*; the date was 1850. Readers were forced each morning to shave to the hundredth psalm groaned out from an impious organ, breakfast was spoiled by a bass trombone belching out a waltz, the morning was ruined by the tinkling of a barrel pianoforte, and so on throughout the rest of the day. The entertainment was brought to a close in late evening by 'a banditti of glee singers'.

A man might have the prettiest house, the sweetest wife, the most unexceptional cook, but all these could be rendered null by 'an endless *charivari*'. And a new terror had arrived to enliven the London scene—the bagpipers. Young boys dressed in kilts carrying pipes roamed the streets searching for houses occupied by expatriate Scotsmen. Two were summoned to Marlborough Street court; they had been told to go away by the collective inhabitants of Suffolk Street, but had refused to do so. There was no law against it, they maintained. The magistrate differed. If they were told to go away, they must go away, he informed

An itinerant musician playing a hurdy-gurdy, once a common sight in London streets

them, fining them a shilling each, and promising them that it would be twenty shillings the next time.

The boys were right in one respect; there was no law to stop them playing, and only if they refused to go away when asked could any action be taken against them. And what was meant by going away? There was sure to be some obstinate creature in one of the houses who maintained that he liked the music, and moving two houses further down could be construed as going away.

Most Londoners put up with it as best as they could, but there were some, from sheer nervous temperament, who could not abide the noise. One of these was the artist John Leech, who was forced to move from his home in Brunswick Square to the quiet suburb of Kensington purely on account of the irritation caused by street musicians. It was admitted by some sufferers that street musicians were not all equally bad; the German bands that appeared during the last half of the century were excellent instrumentalists, and the same could be said of the mixed groups of performers, exiles from professional orchestras for one reason or another, who scratched a living from the pennies thrown to them.

The principal offenders were the purveyors of mechanical music. There were three main sources of mechanical music: the barrel piano, the barrel organ, and the hurdy-gurdy with its derivatives. The first two were pushed, the latter was carried; the hurdy-gurdy had a not disagreeable nasal whine, and compared with the other two instruments, it had little carrying power.

German bands were a prominent feature of Victorian street life, hated by some, adored by others

The Italians held something of a monopoly in barrel-pianos, hiring them from a centre in Clerkenwell. Londoners on holiday on the south coast would have welcomed the appearance of the familiar street instrument (with or without a monkey)

Both the barrel piano and the barrel organ worked on the principle of a revolving cylinder with teeth on them that flicked against tuned strips (for the barrel piano) or opened apertures (for the barrel organ). The tone was loud and coarse. But what was worse for unwilling listeners was the limited repertoire. Barrels were expensive, and it followed that the same tunes would be ground out day in, day out. The effect was of a monstrously amplified ice-cream van.

The centre of the trade was in Clerkenwell, and Italian children were imported into London to take out these instruments for their masters. Occasionally the *dramatis personae* included monkeys, who cavorted about for the benefit of any children or susceptible old ladies. There were many people who loved the organ-grinder. 'The mechanical organs and pianos, which penetrate into the remotest slums and alleys spread musical culture even among the dregs of the people', declared

Working-class girls dancing in the East End streets to the music of a hurdy-gurdy man. The type of dance is interesting, being nearer to the country dance than an urban form. An engraving of 1872

Chambers' Journal in 1881. 'They are, in effect, so many peram-
bulating *conservatoires* teaching the masses the most accepted
music of the day'.

The repertoire of 1881, related the writer, was a wondrous
anthology comprising *La Fille de Madame Angot*, the Row Polka,
'Adeste Fideles', 'Champagne Charlie', the 'Marseillaise', a
sailor's hornpipe, an extract from a Handel oratorio, and the
'Blue Danube' waltz. Proof positive, sums up *Chambers'*
ironically, that we are a nation of music lovers, not like the
Germans, who kick the organ grinder and his associates over
the border, or the French, who compel their street musicians
to wear brass tags.

Although the selections offered by the street organists were
catholic in range, all were reduced to a single tone level by the
unsubtlety of the mechanism, and though the monotonous jangle
of these instruments has today a certain charm, it is not easy to
envisage a London in which it was difficult to get out of earshot
of these monsters. It was music reduced to a norm, but to the
very poor it was the only music they ever heard. There was a
substratum of society that was too low even for the third-rate
music hall.

Most of the operators of barrel organs and barrel pianos were
Italians or Savoyards; by being foreign they avoided the tiresome formality of knowing their place, were immune to insult,
and regarded themselves as victors in a war of attrition. English
vagabond musicians were easily quelled, and patronised into
silence. When they intruded into the world of their betters they
were uneasy, and would scuttle back into the safety of the Seven
Dials or the East End.

It was therefore difficult to take action against the organ
grinders, and any acts against them were instigated by private
people, such as the mathematician, Charles Babbage, who
engaged in a running feud with the breed, gaining some slight
amelioration. The government were reluctant to put acts through
parliament directed at small groups; *laissez-faire* was a way of
life and not just an economic policy, and even those who objected to organ grinders were averse to approving action

A wonderfully evocative photograph of a barrel-piano being played in a main street in the East End of London. For slum dwellers, this was the only music they heard

eliminating the street musician (though it was all right to send children to work at eight years old and have women down the coal mines—these were sanctioned by tradition. *Laissez-faire* operated in the cause of barbarism as well as individual freedom.)

Outdoor music of all kinds was rarely without controversy. Throughout the age, parks and recreation grounds were being opened throughout London to cater for the needs of the poor, and in 1856 Sunday bands were permitted in these parks, much to the distress of the Lord's Day Observance Society and their supporters such as the Earl of Shaftesbury. This move to introduce what he called a Parisian Sunday coincided with the decision to consider opening the Crystal Palace on Sunday. When the Earl of Shaftesbury heard of something that affronted his religious sensibilities he reacted in two ways: he prayed, and he organised opposition. As he had, in 1847, stopped the delivery of mail on

Outdoor music could be strange but hardly ever as surrealist as seen in this engraving of 1885

a Sunday, no doubt he considered prayer was efficacious.

To stop bands playing in the parks on a Sunday, Shaftesbury had the help of a puppet group, the Working Men's Lord's Day Rest Association, but meetings chaired by Shaftesbury were sabotaged and the opposition, founded on the axiom that their political liberties were more secure under the charter of the Sabbath than any king-given charter, foundered. The general public, considering Shaftesbury the voice of crabbed puritanism, laid siege to his house, but they need not have worried. The future of bands in the park was never in doubt.

Sunday for the poor was a day of entertainment and music. The better-off suffered Sunday, tacitly agreeing with the motto 'Ennui was born in London on a Sunday', and, for the sake of their servants, upheld it as a day of rest. The rich were pragmatic; to avoid the London Sunday they made off to the country or the seaside for the weekend.

The taboo against enjoying oneself on Sunday was detrimental to the progress of many musical projects such as choral and band work. In the 1850s a half-day off on Saturday was an exception rather than the rule, and Sunday was the only time for practising. The increasing interest in brass bands put many Christians of a nonconformist hue into a quandary; should they lay up their instruments on the day of rest, or should they seize the opportunity to practise?

Was the prejudice against public music on a Sunday inspired

The bandstand in Vauxhall Gardens, renowned for its concerts and open-air dancing. It closed in 1859 in response to the growing mood of repression

A fair at the Licensed Victuallers' Asylum in London in 1845, an interesting early example of a military band employed to play at an open-air function

purely by religious motives? It seems not. One of the opposition to music in the park was Edward Baines, a Leeds MP with cotton interests, who wrote a pamphlet on the subject in which he states:

> The love of music is all but universal: in itself it is innocent and lawful, but it may be used for the worst purposes, as well as for the best. The strains of martial music cause the pulse to bound, and fire the imagination, and they are wholly out of accordance with the sacred repose of the Sabbath.

He also believed that music in the parks would invite civil disturbance. Baines was at one with other industrialists in fearing the mob. The working classes massed in London parks, pulses bounding as they listened to military band music; who knows what they would not do? As it happened, he need not have worried. The most eager audience was the respectable lower middle classes.

Brass bands were basically an open air movement. They were primarily works' bands, supported by enlightened employers who wished to keep their operatives out of the gin palaces. The Stalybridge Old Band dates back to 1814, the Black Dyke Mills Band to 1816, and although the movement took some time to get into its stride, by the 1830s it was beginning to assume significant proportions. A number of factors helped it on its way, the most important of which was the introduction of the versatile cornet à piston. In the north of England Herbert Milburn was building up enthusiasm, and *The Cornopean*, a magazine devoted to the interests of the cornet player, known as cornopeans or cornopheans, began publishing cornet solos with piano accompaniment. Small travelling groups such as the Distin family moved about the industrial towns of the north as a brass sextet.

The interest of industrialists in supporting brass bands was not solely altruistic. The Chartist movement formed after the 1832 Reform Bill had, in 1838, led to riots and large-scale civil disobedience in Birmingham, and it was felt advisable to direct the attentions of the working classes into calmer fields. Anxiety for the future was also responsible for the spread of Mechanics' Institutes throughout the large cities, and by 1841 two hundred had been established.

Music would utilise excess energy, and music was included in the curriculum of the Mechanics' Institute. But there was music and music, as Sir John Herschel pointed out in his *Manual for Mechanics' Institutes* (1839):   •

> Music and dancing (the more's the pity) have become so closely associated with ideas of riot and debauchery among the less cultivated classes, that a taste for them, for their own sakes, can hardly be said to exist, and before they can be recommended as innocent or safe amusements, a very great change of ideas must take place.

One of the largest of the Mechanics' Institute was in Manchester, and eighty-four men enrolled in their vocal class, but

The AB Kettleby Brass Band in the 1890s

many working men considered singing too effeminate. Singing also lacked the element of competition. On the other hand, brass bands were ideally suited to the competitive spirit, and from small beginnings such as the Burton Constable contest in which four bands took part, brass band competitions proliferated, until, after the success of a competition at the Great Exhibition of 1851, a centre was set up at Belle Vue, Manchester, in 1853.

The movement of brass bands across country was greatly facilitated by the new railway system, which was considerably more advanced in the north than it was in the south. It was possible to travel sixty miles and return home for 2/6. This was an important point when one considers the low value of the prizes that were to be won at competitions; the first prize at Belle Vue was £16. The travelling expenses were often paid by the company, which frequently purchased the band instruments as well. There were sometimes provisos—the members of the band were to be non-drinking, and although occasional insobriety was ignored, this feature was acknowledged in the titles of bands, the Leeds Temperance Band, for example.

Competitions not only prevented brass bands from getting stale, from pottering along without external criticism, but also permitted the individual members to get some inkling of what the world was like outside their own townships. In an indirect way, by recommendation and word of mouth, this facilitated mobility of labour between the industrial cities and towns of the midlands and the north. The patronage of employers also helped form a bridge between capital and labour, and where brass bands were numerous there were few strikes.

Brass bands had an edge over conventional orchestras in that they were more suited to outdoor work. Circuses, zoos, seaside resorts, all realised this. Brass bands could also 'carry' inexperienced players who would stick out like a sore thumb in an orchestra of mixed string, wind and brass. Although there cannot be the wealth of tone colour in a brass band as there is in an orchestra, this was of minor importance compared with ensemble playing and efficient presentation.

It was fortunate that brass bands arrived on the national scene when a repertoire was being opened for them by the activities of Jullien and his contemporaries at the promenade concerts. Jullien travelled widely round the country, and the brass band musicians eagerly attended his concerts, marvelling at the feats of his cornet player, Herr Koenig. Jullien made the brass band world aware of a range of works especially suited to their medium—not his quadrilles, waltzes and polkas, which were mediocre when divorced from the composer's presence, but the overtures of Auber, Boieldieu, Adam and Herold. These formed a prime element in the brass band repertoire, and still do. Brisk, gay, tuneful, they go well in brass band arrangements.

Gradually brass bands became big business. Between 1862 and 1871 one band won nearly £1,500 at contests. Interest was aroused in the south of England, and in 1861 the band of the London Volunteer Corps secured a second prize at a contest, a feat that would have been inconceivable a decade earlier. With large sums of money changing hands, a good deal of chicanery entered into the contests; judges were accused of favouritism, there were near riots when unpalatable decisions were made,

HIGHAM'S (THE FAMOUS 1ST MANCHESTER VOLS) BAND IN 188

Higham's Band of 1881, *a military looking group with Teutonic overtones*

and bandsmen guarded their instruments with their lives in case they were tampered with.

The sign of a movement having arrived is the production of a magazine. The *Brass Band News* was started in 1881, and the subsequent two decades saw the brass band movement at its peak. At Belle Vue in 1888, thirty-five bands played to an audience of 8,000. In 1857 the test piece, which all contestants were obliged to play, was the 'Londesborough Galop', a piece that merely demanded that the band play together in reasonable tune. In 1888 it was the overture to Wagner's *The Flying Dutchman*, a difficult work by any standard.

Other competitions were contending with Belle Vue for the leading role. In 1895 there were 222 brass band contests throughout Britain, many of them offering considerable monetary rewards to the winner, and attended by a knowledgeable public. No amateur movement in music had established itself with such vigour, and although brass bands had been used as ancillaries at Jullien's concerts, they were almost totally ignored by musical commentators

Nevertheless, the versatility of the brass ensemble had been recognised by organisations such as the Salvation Army, and small brass bands were used to herald their street processions and accompany their street-corner devotions. Some of the effects of the brass band movement were predicted by those who deplored working class participation in music—brass bands were often at the head of columns of strikers.

The role of the brass band in providing public entertainment was restricted because most of the players were employees of companies who backed the bands. These firms, though appreciative of the prestige brought to them by a successful band, drew the line at pure philanthropy. Bandsmen were workers first, musicians second. The military bands, who offered entertainment of a similar kind at spas, watering places, and at bandstands in the parks, had no such restrictions. In the 1850s military bands were diligently promoted by the various regiments, and though their historical role was to accompany the fighting men into battle, this was secondary to raising morale and for ceremonial purposes.

In 1860 there was a standing army in Britain of 100,000 men,

An open-air band concert at Wimbledon in 1871

and most regiments of standing had their own band. There was kudos to be obtained from playing to a civil audience, and there was competition between the regiments as to which could raise the best bands. The bands of the Royal Artillery and Grenadier Guards augmented promenade concerts in 1871. Like brass bands, the make-up of the military band made it an all-weather outfit, and shivering holiday-makers in Scarborough could relieve their boredom by listening to a military band suffering under the English weather as they themselves were. Bournemouth went one better; from 1876 they had a military band of sixteen players, all of whom had been in the Italian army and wore the uniform.

CHAPTER FOURTEEN

COUNTRY MATTERS

In 1898 the folk-song collector and enthusiast Cecil Sharp gave a lecture at the Hampstead Conservatoire in which he claimed that the melodies of the great masters, Mozart, Beethoven and Schubert included, were scarcely to be mentioned in the same breath with the ditties of rustic Somerset. The composer Arnold Bax was at this lecture, and he commented that the folk-song phase was inevitably followed up by an enthusiasm for folk dancing. 'As to this infliction', he declared, 'I, for one, would have been happy to cry: "Their nine men's morris is choked up with mud".'

Our knowledge of folk song in Victorian times is cluttered up by inessentials. The response of Arnold Bax to the late nineteenth-century involvement in folk song was shared by many professional musicians and music critics, who saw young incompetent composers plundering the folk song repertoire, and making tedious use of the mannerisms they found there—the use of modes and the minor seventh (play a scale on the piano beginning on D and ending on D using just the white notes and you have, for example, the Dorian mode). Ernest Newman called this preoccupation with folk song 'solemn wassailing round the village pump'.

One of the major barriers to full comprehension of Victorian folk song lies in the inability or unwillingness to report it accurately. Musicians who went in search of folk song, more in duty-bound than pleasure, saw folk music as essentially a bastard version of art music. Any irregularities needed to be ironed out to make it fit in with orthodox music, and the quaint features, such as the tunes being in a mode and not a recognised key, had to be regularised by adding a sharp here or removing a flat there. It was also thought necessary to tidy up the shape of the tunes; asymmetrical airs had to be chopped into regular eight-bar periods. It was too readily assumed that the singer was at fault in his rendering, a natural assumption, as by the time systematic research was being carried out in the field in the 1890s, pure folk song had been in a long decline and the singers were old and doddery.

Was folk song in the nineteenth century a pseudo-popular music? Many of the investigators liked to think so, preferring the image of dedicated men and women embalming a dying cause in their notebooks to that of people who were short-changed by a mildly hostile rustic population. Sharp had doubts about the efficacy of the collectors. 'Intimacy with a peasant may go a long way', he declared, 'and yet stop short of his songs'.

It does not need much imagination to visualise how the country people felt, being referred to as peasants. Inarticulate the countryman may have been, but he was the reverse of stupid. One researcher, Frank Kidson, published two volumes of col-lected songs in the 1890s called *English Peasant Songs* and *Songs of the North Countrie*, and although his niece protested that this was the publisher's idea, this hardly excuses the mixture of patronage and Merrie England *schmalz* that dogs not only Kidson —a diligent careful worker—but most of his contemporaries.

This was not just the product of the halcyon days of the 'nineties. Between 1855 and 1859 William Chappell (1809-88), a member of the London musical firm of Chappell & Co, pub-lished *Popular Music of the Olden Time*, an expansion of a collection of 'national English airs' made by him between 1838 and 1840, a project that led to him founding the Musical Antiquarian Society. Chappell was a pioneer in this field, and there was some excuse for his editing and formalising. There was some confusion as to what, in the olden time, was art music and folk music. Greatly interested in madrigals, it is certain that his knowledge of these affected his assessment of folk song.

For a long time, Chappell's work was the only attempt to collect and collate. The vogue for glee clubs meant that *Popular Music of the Olden Time* was an indispensable breviary, and although contemporary composers such as Robert Lucas Pearsall (1795-1856) were writing madrigals, preference was given to what were deemed to be authentic vocal works of the sixteenth and seventeenth centuries.

Performers readily believed that folk music was a half-educated reflection of art music, for Chappell, by ironing out any aesthetic dissonance, had pre-empted the situation. A new edition of *Popular Music of the Olden Time*, published in 1893, greatly influenced the new school of folk-song collectors. In an artistic chaos, Chappell was the only beacon to be seen, and because he was writing and collecting in an age when the old music was uncorrupted by the invasion of the industrial revolution, then he must have more authority.

Frank Kidson was one of the first on the scene in the revival of interest in folk song, a phrase that was not current until the second half of the nineteenth century. He had articles published by local newspapers in 1886 on old songs. In 1889 the Reverend S. Baring-Gould published his *Songs of the West*. Since 1872, when he had inherited the family estate in Devon, Baring-Gould had been stomping over the west country collecting folk songs, myths, and tales of ghoul and werewolf, revamping them for a popular audience. Occasionally he interspersed his researches with a novel. Until Cecil Sharp, he was the most read of the popularisers, but being a civilized squarson it was not to be expected that he would take down his material cold. When he heard 'Strawberry Fair' in a Devon pub he liked the tune, but said later, 'The text is unsuitable and I've been constrained to re-write it'. Once a man has made a statement like that it is difficult to treat him as a fount of accuracy.

The researchers were happy to take down the tunes as they heard them, willing to take a stand against the musical experts who advised them to refashion the melody to suit a late Victorian audience. There was no moral dilemma there. With the words it was an entirely different matter, for there was no question about it—the rustics, like the rude licentious soldiery of our own age, were fond of dirty songs.

This was contrary to the image. In 1899, at the first annual meeting of the Folk Song Society, Sir Hubert Parry lauded folk song as a wholesome alternative to modern popular song, which he associated with jerry building, sham jewellery, shoddy clothes, gin palaces, fish shops—everything that Freudian word association tests would bring to mind by the mention of 'music hall'. Not so with folk song. Parry wrote:

> It grew in the heart of the people before they devoted themselves so assiduously to the making of quick returns; and it grew there because it pleased them to make it, and because what they made pleased them; and that is the only way good music is ever made.

Parry was a typical professional musician of his time. Thoroughly out of touch with the people who produced the songs he was enthusing over—his only departure from academic groves was a brief spell at Lloyd's—his conception of non-urban life evolved around yokels with straw in their mouths, good fellows none the less, and buttercups and daisies. The music hall songs were packed with innuendo and encouraged free-living; Marie Lloyd was no better than she ought to be; the promenades at the back of the music halls reflected the lasciviousness of the stage, the vulgarity of the music, and the animal mentality of the audience. He did not attempt to reconcile the cool limpid melodies of folk song with their less than pure words; he did not even know about it, though this did not prevent him addressing the Folk Song Society.

Parry shared the illusion that folk song was there for the benefit of a benevolent middle class. It was not. Folk song dealt with the issues that concerned country people—contemporary events that affected them, work, and sex, the last two frequently being combined, so that sex is expressed in work terms by analogy and punning, as in the following song:

> It's a gentleman soldier, in a sentry he did stand,
> He fell in love with a fair maid, and boldly took her hand;
> He kindly did salute her, he kissed her in a joke,
> He drilled her into a sentry box, wrapt up in a soldier's
> cloak.

Baring-Gould could not believe his ears when he was in the field collecting material, and preferred to consider that the singers had no realisation of the double meanings, though the following is explicit enough to anyone without blinkers:

> As I walked out one spring morning fair,
> To view the fields and take the air,
> There I heard a pretty maid making her complain,
> And all she wanted was the chiefest grain, the chiefest grain.
> I said to her: 'My pretty maid,
> Come tell me what you stand in need'.
> 'Oh yes, kind sir, you're the man to do my deed,
> For to sow my meadow with the wanton seed, the wanton
> seed'.

This is a common theme, the casual rustic encounter leading to sex. The song below was collected by the broadsheet printers, and put out by William Pratt, of 82 Digbeth, Birmingham, 'the cheapest Song Warehouse in England'. Despite its provenance, it is a typical country ditty:

> As I walked out one morning I met a buxom lass,
> Belonging to a dairy man, she had a field of grass,
> It grew between two mountains at the foot of a rising hill,
> She bade me to cut it down while the birds did sweetly sing.
> She said, my lusty young man, will you now begin
> My grass is in good order, I long to have it down,
> It is such pleasant weather I long to clear the ground,
> So get your scythe in order to mow my meadow down.

A woman's body in terms of landscape was an often repeated theme, not only in folk song but in urban jokes. The London district named Mount Pleasant was always good for a laugh. Husbandry and sex lent themselves to endless variations, and the generic title 'The Mower' may cover dozens of similar songs. The following is identical in mood and vocabulary to the one above:

As I was a-walking on the fourteenth of July,
I met a maid and I asked her age, she made me this reply:
'I have a little meadow I've keeped for you in store,
And it's only due I should tell you true, he never was mowed
    before.'
She said: 'My handsome young man, if a mower that you be,
I'll give you good employment if you'll come along with me.'
So it was my good employment to wander up and down
With my taring scythe all to contrive to mow her meadow
    down.

Small wonder that Cecil Sharp felt reluctant to include such dangerous matter, though he regretted it. 'In a few instances', he wrote in *Folksongs from Somerset*, 'the sentiment of the song has

The ballad-sellers were a link between town and country that existed well into the 1870s. They not only sold bawdy urban ballads to country people but sang or played tunes that they had heard in the countryside to the ballad-printers in the towns, who gave these airs new words and sent them on their way again, refurbished

been softened, because the conventions of our less delicate and more dishonest time demand such treatment'.

Francis Child (1825-96) was affronted by the earthy. A Harvard professor of Early English and Anglo-Saxon, his annotated Spenser was followed by *English and Scottish Ballads* (1857-59), a massive eight volume collection. Child was no easily satisfied dilettante, and scholarly etiquette compelled him to go on even when his sensibility was offended. There were certain kinds of songs which were, said Child, 'veritable dunghills in which, only after a great deal of sickening grubbing, one finds a very moderate jewel'.

During the time Child was researching, there was a good deal of two-way traffic relating to folk song. The ballad printers of the towns were absorbing genuine folk material, revamping it or spicing it up, and sending it back by way of itinerant musicians and ballad vendors. The doyen of this lively but unsavoury crew was James Catnach, who bought an old wooden press in 1813 and proceeded to print and publish in broadsheet form:

> ballads, battledores, lotteries, primers, doubtful scandals, fabulous duels between ladies of fashion, cooked assignations, sudden deaths of eminent individuals, apocryphal elopements, real or *catchpenny* accounts of murders, impossible robberies, delusive suicides, manufactured crimcons, dark deeds, local *fauxpas*, and public executions.

These ballads and songs were printed on single sheets of paper, and sold for a half-penny or a penny by the thousand. At the head of the sheet was the legend 'To the tune of . . .' These were usually traditional airs which everyone knew, and when the ballads had been assimilated into the country repertoire, local jargon and dialect reshaping the text, it is not to be wondered at that in thirty or forty years time collectors would accept them as the genuine article. Most of the songs and ballads that reached the country people were soon dead, but with the vast amount of titles issued—one publisher advertised 'upwards of five thousand different sorts of ballads'—some were bound to survive.

The more sensational titles sold not by the thousand but by

the hundred thousand. A case that received the plaudits of the masses was Maria Marten and the Red Barn, and according to Henry Mayhew 1,650,000 copies of the ballad on this theme were sold. Maria Marten remained in folk mythology throughout the nineteenth century, yet it was merely a rather sordid murder. Maria Marten was seduced and murdered at Polsted in Suffolk in 1827 by a man named Corder, who hid the body in a solitary building called the Red Barn. At the trial, the stepmother of the deceased gave testimony that she had received knowledge of the hiding place in a dream, and Corder was brought to trial at Bury St Edmunds in 1828.

The deliberate manufacture of folk song by Catnach and others did much to confuse the enthusiasts, and although Catnach himself died in 1841, his business was kept going for a good deal longer. In the 1860s the *National Review* declared that the ballad singer was disappearing; but this was in London. In the provinces the broadside vendors were still active.

The picture is even more confused by large numbers of art songs masquerading as folk. Theo Marzials' *Twickenham Ferry* has the outward lineaments of folk-song:

O-hoi-ye-ho! Ho-ye-ho! Who's for the ferry?
(The briar's in bud, the sun's going down)
It's late as it is and I haven't a penny,
And how shall I get me to Twickenham town?

This would not have taken in an experienced collector, but there were border-line cases, and it would have been a bold man who would have signed his reputation away on the authenticity of the 'Skye Boat Song' (it is phoney).

Nevertheless it was the broadside printers who presented the major threat to a true evaluation of the genuine folk song. Catnach issued 14,000 ballads of one sort or another. He paid men to collect ballads from singers in country inns, and was therefore only doing on a business footing what the enthusiasts were doing for love. The actual blending of tune and words was done in an appropriately folksy way. He employed a fiddler on his premises

The notorious London district of Seven Dials, the home of the broadside printers. These much maligned printers helped to keep folk song going when it was in danger of being lost and forgotten

in the Seven Dials, and ballad writers and singers who came to see him could work at the tune on the spot while Catnach would listen to see if it would work.

How could the purist deal with broadsides issued by the London press that accurately presented real folk songs? Henry Such of Union Street, The Borough, had in his list such songs as 'The foggy dew', 'The trees they do grow high', 'Seventeen come Sunday', the acknowledged classics of the genre. But for the axiom that commercial exploitation of folk song was immoral, it may be said that in such instances the London printers were doing posterity a service.

Many folk song collectors had a fixation about the superiority of the oral tradition, and would travel miles to hear a seventy year old man croaking out a song that he may well have picked up from a London broadside fifty years earlier. In the pursuit of the oral tradition the wife of a colonel, Ella Leather, went to work in the hop fields, her ears pricked for the authentic voice of old England; Miss Laura Smith ventured life and honour in searching for sailors' songs in the slums of Tyneside. The refusal of some of the country people to sing some of the bawdier songs to the gentry who called with their notebooks was reckoned a success rather than a failure, for the oral tradition retained thereby its mystique.

Folk music differs from art music in that it can exist for use rather than entertainment. The most obvious example of folk song in the service of man is the sea shanty, where the rhythms bear an intimate correlation with the movements of sailors hauling ropes, etc, and song was widely used in industrial circumstances that demanded manual co-ordination, such as mining. In rural work, the combination of numbers of men engaged in one specific activity, where muscular integration is necessary, is not so common. In the heyday of steam farming a hundred years ago, where great stationary steam engines hauling ploughs and other implements across fields using lines and fixed anchors needed a work force of more than a dozen men, then song was used as a co-ordinator.

On the land, song was chiefly used as a diversion. This particularly applied when boring communal tasks needed to be carried out, such as potato-picking, hop-picking, or pea-picking. When sexes were mixed there was more inclination to opt for bawdy songs (an analogy is the dirty joke which in mixed company acts as a sexual attack by proxy). The kind of allusive song replete with agricultural and horticultural metaphor was ideal for this purpose. When women were working together without the presence of men there would be a preference for songs of love, which were usually a trifle sad, revolving on jilting and premature death.

The story ballads played minor roles in the working life of country people, being reserved for social occasions. In the pubs the ballads would undergo mutations, and local celebrities would be inserted into the text, replacing the names of those who were of little interest to the locals. Ballads were used as set pieces by farm workers who felt that they had a voice.

Unquestionably the folk-song tradition was stronger than most of the purists thought, and although there were aspects that had all but died out—farm labourers no longer crooned to the growing wheat and the rural deities were forgotten—folk song as it was and not as it should be was continually being enlivened by new blood. The massive immigration of Irish working men to act as navvies in the late eighteenth and early nineteenth century or on railway construction in the nineteenth century brought an infusion of Irish folk melody into areas that had been anthropologically and musically barren. The railways and the canals penetrated deep into the vitals of folk-song country, and whether the Irish were passing through or putting down roots, the effect on the native song was considerable, especially as Irish folk song was complementary to English folk song, using many of the same devices—the minor seventh, a definite modal sound, and a melody contained within a small compass.

Folk song was not only affected by the intrusion of the travelling ballad vendors and singers. The railway system brought mobility to country people. In 1843 there were 1,775 miles of track in England and Wales, in 1861, 7,820, and in 1879, 12,547. Most farm workers did not take advantage of the railway, but some did. The 1851 Great Exhibition brought many country people to London who had never before been out of their county, and in the pubs and music halls of the metropolis they were confronted with a new kind of music, elements of which they took back home, thereby enhancing their social stature.

Country life was close and familiar; farm labourers ate their meals with their employers, and tenant farmers did not consider it beneath their dignity to work for yeoman farmers. There was pressure on yeoman farmers to introduce a note of gentility into their environment; this might merely mean the introduction of a piano into the parlour and the infliction of singing or dancing lessons on daughters, but nevertheless these produced a different aural experience, and farm workers were bound to have some acquaintance with drawing-room song and popular airs from

1830s and 1840s English opera such as 'Home, Sweet Home' and 'I dreamt that I dwelt in marble halls'.

Although pure folk song went into decline during the Victorian age, there were sufficient new influences to keep it healthy and kicking. This was not true of folk dancing, though a distinction must be made between country dancing and folk dancing. A characteristic account of country dancing can be found in Francis Kilvert's diaries of October 1871:

> As I write I hear the scraping and squealing of the fiddle and the ceaseless heavy tramp of the dancers as they stamp the floor in a country dance.

There is another account dated 11 November 1871:

> As I passed the house I heard music and dancing, the people dancing at the wedding. They were dancing in an upper room, unfurnished, tramp, tramp, tramp, to the jingling of a concertina, the tramping was tremendous. I thought they would have brought the floor down. They seemed to be jumping round and round. When I came back the dance seemed to have degenerated into a romp and the girls were squealing, as if they were being kissed or tickled and not against their will.

Dancing of this nature was a rough and ready business. Improvised square dances combined with bucolic versions of popular dances of the time such as the waltz and polka. In rustic weddings and functions there were always women who had been domestic servants at the great houses in the district, and who had observed fashionable balls and had been participants in the servants' balls which were great features of country house life. Anything would do provided that it was lively. The ceremony and ritual of the authentic folk dance was utterly remote from such beanos.

Folk dance involved propitiation, worship, thanksgiving, commemoration. Its survival depended on the belief that somehow the bounty of the land lay in the laps of rural gods, that by making some outward sign there would be good harvests and the cattle would not die. As the century went on, country people were less and less inclined to believe in unseen forces, leaving such idle speculation to their literary betters such as Thomas Hardy. Their livelihood was dependent on more mundane things—the buying price of wheat, what bullocks were getting in the cattle market, and the topsy-turvy round of inflation and deflation—and they knew it.

Such a phenomenon as the Horn Dance at Abbot's Bromley, held every September, in which men wore antlers and were believed to be commemorating the restoration of forest rights during the reign of Henry III, was not only atavistic but incomprehensible. And why was there morris dancing in the Thaxted streets every Easter Monday? Country people did not know nor did they care.

Morris dancing may be taken as the epitome of the true folk dance. Popular in the sixteenth century, it came to Britain via France (the Morisque) and Spain (the Morisco) from the Moors, and was united with an older indigenous pageant dance performed at various times in honour of Robin Hood. It came to

Country dancers of the type shown here took their lives in their hands when they ventured into the city slums. Traditions had long been forgotten, and morris dancers and their ilk were subjects for fun and ribaldry

have less and less significance as the centuries went by, and by the time of Charles I, morris dancers were paid entertainers who performed at Christmas, whereas formerly Whitsuntide had been the favoured season.

Certain counties kept morris dancing going into the nineteenth century. These included Hertfordshire, Herefordshire, Gloucestershire, Somerset and Wiltshire, and the home counties. The appearance of Hertfordshire morris dancers in Goswell Street, London, in 1826, was sufficiently rare to arouse comment. In 1854 there were still morris dancers in Northamptonshire, a county that retained its hold on the past longer than most (witches were extant there until the 1880s), and Oxfordshire morris dancers were observed in the 1860s, though they had relinquished the full costume and were rigged up with a few ribbons.

In all these instances, the appearances were uncommon, and towns which had their own specialities, such as Thaxted or Helston (the furry-dance bowdlerised into the 'Floral Dance', an art song) were considered curios. The injection of new life into folk dancing by dedicated folklorists was disinternment rather than rejuvenation, and any claims that they were preventing old customs from dying out should be discounted.

CHAPTER FIFTEEN

THE ECONOMICS OF VICTORIAN POPULAR MUSIC

IN POPULAR MUSIC the promoting and packaging is often as important as the product, and this was as true a century ago as it is today. In drawing-room ballads the driving force was the publishers who subsidised ballad concerts and gave singers a royalty for pushing their material. In music hall song there was a wide variety of entrepreneurs. In street music there were the mini-tycoons who rented out barrel pianos to the vagabond musicians at so much a day. Even in serious music, business men were behind the scenes. The publishing house of Novello promoted Promenade Concerts at the Albert Hall, Chappell's initiated and financed the building of St James's Hall, Piccadilly, in 1858, and although it seemed at first as though it would be a white elephant —an expensive white elephant as it cost £70,000 instead of the anticipated £23,000—the extensive series of popular concerts held there proved immensely profitable.

Chappell's interest in giving London a new concert hall was not wholly altruistic (though the family played a great part in London musical life). The St James's Hall was a display centre for Chappell pianos, Chappell music, and Chappell artists. Tom Chappell also persuaded Charles Dickens to give readings under

*St James's Hall was built in 1858, and financed by Chappell, the
music publishers and piano makers, for the presentation of their songs,
their singers, and their pianos. Paderewski made his first appearance at
St James's Hall*

his auspices, and Dickens responded—made wealthy by this
branching away from pure literature—by saying

> I do believe that such people as the Chappells are very rarely
> to be found in human affairs . . . Everything is done for me
> with the utmost liberality and consideration. Every want I
> can have on these journeys is anticipated, and not the
> faintest mark of the tradesman spirit ever peeps out.

Dickens also stated that the Chappells were speculators,
though of the worthiest and most honourable kind. Speculation

paid off. The purchase of the publishing rights in Balfe's *The Bohemian Girl* was shrewd and well-timed, as was the Chappell interest in Gounod's *Faust* after they had observed how well a sung rather than acted version had gone in the music hall. More profitable than either of these two ventures was the publishing of the Gilbert and Sullivan operas; Tom Chappell also helped finance the original D'Oyly Carte enterprise, and when William Boosey joined his firm in 1894, with a background of drawing-room ballad presentation, Chappell's had a benevolent grasp over the whole of London music. Their influence was wholly for the good of music.

In serious music, behind the scenes deals and manipulations could frequently work to the detriment of music. Henry Wylde was more of an administrator than a composer. Born in 1822, he soon put himself in positions where he could exert influence and sponsor his own music. He was on the jury in the musical instrument section of the Great Exhibitions of 1851 and 1862, was Professor of Music at Gresham College, London, in 1863, founded the London Academy of Music and was responsible for the building of St George's Hall, Langham Place, in 1867. He was behind the formation of the New Philharmonic Society in 1852, assumed control of it in 1858 and conducted its annual series of concerts until 1879.

With this background, it is not surprising that his own works were heard more often than their worth warranted. Berlioz had also been a jury member in the musical instrument section of the Great Exhibition in 1851, and perhaps it is no coincidence that in 1852 he was the conductor of the New Philharmonic Society orchestra and that one of the works played was a concerto by Wylde. It was the you-scratch-my-back-I'll-scratch-yours syndrome in High Art. Fortunately the music critics were not in the club. Wylde's concerto, according to *The Athenaeum*, was 'fit only for a RA concert or other training arena', despite the programme note declaring that Dr Wylde 'held a recognised position amongst the ablest musical professors of the day'.

Hullah and Curwen, with their Sol-fa Systems, were able to sponsor composers of their choice. The conductor/composer

Costa unremittingly advanced the fortunes of his oratorio *Eli*,
and the ·Harmonic Union, formed in 1852, would be the last
ensemble to ignore the music of its conductor, Julius Benedict.
When Benedict was conductor at the Drury Lane Theatre, he
made certain that two of his operas were in the repertoire. It
would be a matter of indifference if the works of Wylde, Costa,
and Benedict were up to standard, but it is clear that their
places in the sun were won purely on account of the extra-
musical influence of their composers.

It was prestige rather than money that drove these composers.
There was a great deal of money to be made in Victorian music,
but the composers were low on the list of recipients compared
with publishers, performers, management and backers. Publishers did well on music-hall songs, drawing-room ballad, and
popular instrumental music, plus miscellaneous works such as
piano tutors. Management could be a precarious business. Mr
Gye, the manager of Covent Garden, enjoyed profits averaging
£15,000 a year between 1872 and 1878. Despite its ups and
downs, opera was a surprisingly consistent money-spinner, for
although costs of production were high, this was countered by
admission charges that were prohibitive to all except the rich,
and poor pay for all except the principals. At Covent Garden
there was a chorus of thirty-two women and forty-two men,
costing the management £140 a week.

Drawing-room ballads provided a steady income. The writers
of the lyrics made no great fortunes, and many were not paid at
all, their words having been plundered from other sources. The
writers who did best were those who were intimately associated
with composers who commanded high fees, Fitzball with
Bishop, for example. Bishop refused £500 for the copyright
of his song 'My Pretty Jane', made popular by Sims Reeves, an
all-round singer who went wherever the pickings were greatest.
On the other hand, Charles Mackay, who wrote songs for the
song and supper rooms which were upgraded for drawing-room
use, sold his songs for a pound apiece. When he was in America
he sold his song 'Woodman, Spare That Tree!' for two dollars.
Instrumental music came in all shapes and sizes, arrangements

The Empire Theatre, Leicester Square, formerly the Pandora, was opened as a straight theatre in 1884, but soon went over to music hall. A feature of the Empire was its promenade, and in 1894 a number of worthy ladies tried to have the theatre's licence rescinded because prostitutes were using the promenade as their beat. A partition was erected, soon torn down by the swells of the period, including the young Winston Churchill

for various combinations of popular ballads subsidising more worthy music. Piano music of the preceding age—it must be remembered that Beethoven did not die until 1827—sold in reasonable quantities, and made money by virtue of the fact that production costs were low, the engraved plates being ready for reprinting any time. Unprofitable music was balanced by Mendelssohn's *Songs Without Words* and meretricious fantasies on popular airs.

One will never know whether the publication of oratorio broke even. The cost of printing new oratorios whose par for the course was one performance must be countered with the turnover of *The Messiah* and *Elijah*, especially when Tonic Sol-fa and other Sol-fa systems made this music in Sol-fa notation a viable business proposition. One suspects that many publishers printed oratorios as a moral duty rather than as a way of making money; the number of parts and the length pushed up production costs, though the individual members of amateur choral societies could club together to buy the scores.

The field that was widest open for money-making was music hall. In 1878 there were 347 licensed in London. The various managements vied with each other for the top celebrities. When the 'Great' Macdermott caused such a stir by singing 'We Don't Want to Fight' at the London Pavilion his salary was ten pounds a week, and was immediately increased to twenty pounds a week. His sudden fame made him worth sixty pounds a week in the provinces, and for a Manchester pantomime he got a hundred and sixty pounds a week. Cissie Loftus, a music hall mimic made a cult figure by Max Beerbohm, commanded two hundred and fifty pounds a week, Marie Lloyd a hundred and fifty pounds a week and upwards. The wage bill of one of the large London halls could approach £1,000 a week.

These were staggering production costs for the period, and they could only be met by full houses and a good bar. The 'wet money' helped to lift the profits considerably. As has been mentioned before, the Act of Suitability of 1878 weeded out the small halls, but the survivors, bigger and more opulent than anything that had gone before, found no shortage of backers. Music hall was a gilt-edged investment.

Managements were acutely aware of the value of advertisement, and in the West End music halls between seventy and a hundred free seats were handed out to newspapers and periodicals for new shows, leading up to the setting-up of a shop in Drury Lane, nominally a barber's which took in these complimentary tickets for a consideration and resold them at about a third of the face value.

A large number of periodicals were published dealing with the music hall; not surprisingly, many of these periodicals were managed by music hall proprietors. The first of these papers was the *Era*, originally an organ for licensed victuallers, run by Charles Hibble, the manager of the Sheridan Knowles, a tavern saloon in Brydges Street, Covent Garden. The *Magnet*, started in 1866, was the first paper to run a professional directory of variety halls in the country. The *London Entr'acte* boasted a circulation of 20,000 a week; one of its pages was a specific music hall programme, and the periodical was sold in that particular music hall as a programme and periodical combined.

The *Music Hall Critic and Programme of Amusements* broke new ground in including interviews with celebrities such as Vance, but staggered on for only seven weeks, and almost as short-lived was the *Artiste*, proprietor James Deacon of Deacon's Music Hall, Clerkenwell. The *Music Hall Gazette* started in the same year (1887), folded almost immediately, and made way for the *Music Hall*. The front man here was a cycling journalist, McWilliams, but the periodical was really in the hands of the music hall singer Charles 'Two Lovely Black Eyes' Coborn.

The music hall theatre in its heyday could absorb almost unlimited funds. The rent of the Lyric Theatre was set at £6,500 a year. But there was never a shortage of 'angels'. For the production of *Charley's Aunt* one backer was so eager to put money into a certain success that, lacking ready cash himself, he borrowed £600 at 60 per cent from a money lender so that he would be sure to get a piece of the cake. Some came unstuck. Lord Londesborough put £11,000 into Boucicault's burlesque *Babil and Bijou*, but Boucicault squandered it all and bolted to America. Boucicault made as much as £40,000 a year.

No institution with the exception of the cinema enjoyed such a meteoric rise as the nineteenth century music hall. In many ways their fortunes have been parallel—small beginnings, a phenomenal growth rate, a rationalisation and the elimination of the little man, followed by a decline as rival forms of entertainment take over. The transitional states of both media (bioscope to cinema, song and supper room to music hall) were confusing, but it took the music hall celebrities longer to realise their potential than the early cinema stars. It was only when the impresarios of the big halls began wooing the song and supper room singers with promises of big money that these possibilities were realised.

Being individualist and independent, the music hall singers could be worked on by guile and flattery. To many, five pounds a week were riches, particularly those who had emerged from the saloons. They needed to join together to establish a norm, but as there did not seem any likelihood of this the managers held the whip hand. Matters would have continued like this, with managers giving as little as they could to their singers.

In the early 1850s it was the custom of a number of music hall managers to meet at the old Coburg Tavern. One of them was Harry Fox, manager of the Mogul. Singers who were working in the provinces often wrote to him to ask if he had any vacancies, and if not, did he know who had. So names were exchanged, and an informal kind of agency was started. About the same time a comic singer, Ambrose Maynard, had the idea of compiling a register of performers which could be submitted to managers. The performers paid a shilling for this privilege, and although they liked the idea and subscribed, the managers did not, and would have nothing to do with it until one manager was caught on the hop one day and in despair utilised the dreaded agency.

Maynard was instrumental in arranging other dates for performers on his register, and in 1858 opened premises in Waterloo Road. The system Maynard used was known as 'farming'; he would engage the artist at a fixed salary for a fixed period, make contracts with the managers at a higher fee, and pocket the difference, taking a chance that the performer would be in work throughout the period of his contract with him.

The agency profited sufficiently for Maynard to move to better premises in York Road, but in 1865 another agent opened up opposite to him, Charles Roberts. Roberts was instrumental in bringing George Leybourne, the Lion Comique, from Manchester to London and getting his salary raised from £2.10.0 to £120 a week. Roberts charged five per cent for his fee, naming his villa at Kew 'Five Per Cent Villa'.

Many of the agents who proliferated in the 1860s used their business to push their own music hall careers. George Ware started life as a scout for the circus owner Barnum, but in between running an agency he was a writer of popular songs such as 'The Whole Hog or None'. George Sinclair was in an excellent position to be an agent, as he had managed the Bedford Music Hall, and had thus been on the inside looking out. The 'Great' Macdermott once ran an agency in partnership, while W. F. Bushfield had been manager of the Alhambra Music Hall, a comic singer, and the founder of the Magpie Music Hall in Battersea, before trying his hand as an agent.

The agents were in a position to drive hard bargains with management. The lesser artists resented the growing disparity between their salaries and the celebrities, and in an effort to stamp out the middle man they started in 1870 the Music Hall Artistes' Association and Club over a wig shop in Wellington Street, a project that fizzled out within two years. Useful as agents no doubt were to celebrity artist, their effect on London musical life was bad, being responsible in some degree for the closure of small music halls that could not afford the astronomical salaries demanded for the top artists.

The injection of great quantities of money into music hall had mixed results. Investment only went into shows that would produce massive returns; the accent was on lavish productions destined for a long run, and the adventure of the music halls of the 1850s in putting on opera and ballet was to the 1880s and 1890s a mercifully-forgotten eccentricity. On the other hand, patronage was not wholly bad, for the money supporting the Gilbert and Sullivan projects resulted in presentations superbly sung, accompanied and fitted out.

The trend of the last part of the nineteenth century regarding popular music was in giving the public what it wanted and not what it was thought it should have, and this persisted until the first world war. Between the wars there was a set-back to this trend; the music halls were down-graded, and the programmes were directed at the working classes. Popular music was written by professional musicians for a never-never-land in which butlers were common ('Dinner For One, James'), women were fun-loving flappers, or fantasies from musical comedy or the cinema,

and men invariably wore top hats and tails. The lower levels of
society had to make do with this as best as they could.

The composers of popular music had no easily defined audience.
This was altered by the second world war; a nation forcibly
integrated by outside pressure was a much more easily visualised
target for popular song, and there was no vein more readily
pierced than instant nostalgia for the unimaginably desirable pre-
war years. The vacuity of war-time 'Music While You Work'
harks back to the vapidity of the Victorian drawing-room ballad,
and the Forces Programme provided a platform for a radio
equivalent of music hall, such as 'Worker's Playtime'. Appreciation of all kinds of music during the second world war is
reminiscent of the halcyon days of early Victorian England, when
all music was popular, from bawdy ballad to opera and ballet,
when Jullien had his peas rattling in Beethoven's Sixth Symphony
and monster quadrilles blasted the awed ears of the proletariat
and the social layers above, when the great singers of the time
were not worried about wasting their time on 'Home, Sweet
Home'.

In including such subjects as oratorio, ballet and promenade
concerts in a book on popular music it might be thought that this
is stretching the term popular overmuch. But there surely can be
no doubt that to the Victorians all music was popular. Unpopular
music was unthinkable. The man who wiped away a surreptitious
tear after a rendering of 'On the Bridge at Midnight' would
happily go away and laugh uproariously at a parody of it before
going to a Chappell 'Monday Pops' concert or a music at home,
transformed into a Lion Comique for the occasion.

'Have you brought your music?' The Victorians answered
'yes'.

SELECT BIBLIOGRAPHY

Archer, Frank. *An Actor's Notebook* (1911)

Ashton, John. *Century of Ballads* (1887)

Ashton, John. *Modern Street Ballads* (1888)

Ballantine, Serjeant. *Some Experiences* (1882)

Barnett, J. F. *Musical Reminiscences* (1906)

Barton Baker, H. *The London Stage* (1889)

Bennett, A. R. *London in the 1850s and 1860s* (n.d.)

Bennett, Joseph. *Forty Years of Music* (1908)

Benson, E. F. *As We Were* (1930)

Booth, J. B. *Old Pink 'Un Days* (1924)

Booth, J. B. *The Days We Knew* (1943)

Brinsmead, E. *History of the Pianoforte* (1879)

Brookfield, Charles. *Random Reminiscences* (1911)

Burke, T. *Nights in Town* (n.d.)

Burnand, F. C. *Records and Reminiscences* (1903)

Callow, Edward. *Old London Taverns* (1899)

Carse, Adam. *Life of Jullien* (n.d.)

Cavendish, Lady Frederick. *Diary* (1927)

Chambers, Major. *Recollections of a West End Life* (1858)

Chancellor, E. Beresford. *The Pleasure Haunts of London* (1925)

Chorley, H. F. *Thirty Years Musical Recollections* (1862)

Closson, E. *History of the Piano* (1947)

Cox, J. E. *Musical Recollections* (1872)
Craven, Lady Helen. *Notes of a Music Lover* (1897)
Crowest, F. J. *Phases of Musical England* (1881)
Davey, Henry. *History of English Music* (1921)
Davison, J. W. *Music During the Victorian Era* (1912)
Dent, E. J. *Foundation of English Opera* (1928)
Dickens, Charles. *Sketches by Boz* (1850)
Disher, M. Willson. *Winkles and Champagne* (1938)
Edwards, F. G. *Musical Haunts in London* (1895)
Elkin, Robert. *The Old Concert Rooms of London* (1955)
Ellis, S. M. *A Mid-Victorian Pepys* (1923)
Encyclopaedia Britannica. 11th ed. (1910-11)
Felstead, S. T. *Stars Who Made the Halls* (1946)
Forsyth, Cecil. *Music and Nationalism* (1911)
Francillon, R. E. *Mid-Victorian Memories* (n.d.)
Galloway, W. J. *Musical England* (1910)
Gardner, Fitzroy. *More Reminiscences of an Old Bohemian* (n.d.)
Gladstone, Mary, *Diaries and Letters* (1930)
Goldberg, Isaac, *Gilbert and Sullivan* (1935)
Gretton, R. H. *The English Middle Classes* (1917)
Grove, George. *Dictionary of Music and Musicians* (1900 edition)
Gurney, Edmund. *Power of Sound* (1880)
Harrison, Clifford. *Stray Records* (1893)
Haskell, Arnold. *Ballet* (1938)
Haweis, H. R. *Music and Morals* (1871)
Henschel, Sir George. *Musings and Memories* (1918)
Howes, Frank. *English Musical Renaissance* (1966)
Howes, Frank. *Folk Music of Britain* (1969)
Hullah, John, *History of Modern Music* (1875)
Hullah, John. *Music in the House* (1878)
Klein, Herman. *Musicians and Mummers* (1925)
Lang, Paul H. *Music in Western Civilization* (1942)
Lee, Edward. *Music of the People* (1970)
Lloyd, A. L. *Folk Song in England* (1967)
Lumley, B. *Reminiscences of the Opera* (1864)
McDonald Rendle, T. *Swings and Roundabouts* (1919)
Mackerness, E. D. *Social History of English Music* (1964)

MacKinlay, Sterling. *Origin and Development of Light Opera* (1927)

McQueen Pope, W. *The Melodies Linger On* (1950)

McQueen Pope, W. *Nights of Gladness* (1956)

Mair, Carlene. *The Chappell Story* (1961)

Maitland, J. A. Fuller. *English Music in the Nineteenth Century* (1902)

Masson, D. *Memories of London in the Forties* (1908)

Morell Holmes, F. *Exeter Hall* (1881)

Nadal, E. S. *Impressions of English Social Life* (1875)

Nettel, Reginald. *The Orchestra in England* (1948)

Nettel, Reginald. *Seven Centuries of Popular Song* (1956)

Ord-Hume, Arthur. *The Player Piano* (1970)

Parry, C. H. *Art of Music* (1893)

Parry, C. H. *Style in Musical Art* (1911)

Ponsonby, Magdalen, *Mary Ponsonby* (1927)

Russell, John F. and Elliot, J. H. *The Brass Band Movement* (1936)

Russell, G. W. E. *Collections and Recollections* (1903)

Sala, G. A. *Twice Round the Clock* (1859)

Sala, G. A. *Living London* (1883)

Scholes, P. A. *Oxford Companion to Music* (1938)

Scholes, P. A. *Mirror of Music 1844-1944* (1947)

Scott, Clement. *Drama of Yesterday and Today* (1899)

Scott, Harold. *The Early Doors* (1946)

Searle, Humphrey, *Ballet Music* (1958)

Shaw, Bernard. *Music in London 1890-94* (1932)

Shaw, Bernard. *London Music 1888-89* (1937).

Shaw, Captain D. *London in the Sixties* (1908)

Shepard, Leslie. *The Broadside Ballad* (1962)

Simpson, Claude M. *British Broadside Ballads* (1966)

Simpson, Harold. *Century of Ballad 1810-1910* (1910)

Stanford, C. V. *Studies and Memories* (1908)

Straus, Ralph. *Sala, a Portrait* (1942)

Stuart, Charles Douglas and Park, A. J. *History of the Variety Stage* (1895)

Tallis, David. *Musical Boxes* (1971)

Walford, Edward. *Old and New London* (1897)

Walker, Ernest. *History of Music in England* (1907)

Ward, Mrs E. M. *Memories of Ninety Years* (n.d.)

Weatherly, Fred E. *Piano and Gown* (n.d.)
Webb, Graham. *Cylinder Musical Box Handbook* (1968)
Webb, Graham. *Disc Musical Box Handbook* (1971)
Wyndham, H. S. *Annals of Covent Garden* (1906)
Young, Percy M. *The Musical Tradition* (1962)

Periodicals and Magazines

All the Year Round
Cassell's Magazine
Chambers' Journal
Choir
English Illustrated Magazine
Household Words
Illustrated London News
Lady's Realm
Leisure Hour
London & Provincial Music Trades Review
London Society
Magazine of Art
Monthly Musical Record
Musical Opinion
Musical Standard
Musical Times
Musical World
Nineteenth Century
Once A Week
Orchestra
Pictorial Times
Pictorial World
Punch
St James Gazette
Saturday Review
Strand
Tonic Sol-fa Reporter
Windsor Magazine

INDEX

A'Beckett, Gilbert, 64, 66, 68
Adam, Adolphe, 28, 169, 201
Agate, James, 157
Albert, Prince Consort, 76, 126, 135, 145, 179
Alboni, Marietta, 149, 150, 152
Anderson, John, 51, 130
Auber, Daniel, 15, 28, 35, 165, 173, 201

Babbage, Charles, 194
Bach, J.S., 138, 143
Baker, Colonel, 50
Balfe, Michael, 28, 91, 128, 129, 159, 161–4, 221
Ball, Edward, 159, 163, 222
BALLADS, 89–95, 161–4, 215–16, 222
Ballantine, Serjeant, 23, 24
BALLET, 12, 13, 28, 35, 36, 124, 165–75
Baring-Gould, S., 207, 209
Barnum, P.T., 227
Bateman, Edgar, 59
Bax, Arnold, 205
Bedford, Duke of, 85
Beecham, Thomas, 133
Beerbohm, Max, 224
Beethoven, Ludwig van, 12, 15, 78, 80, 127, 129, 130, 133, 169, 205, 223, 228
Bell, Graham, 106
Bellini, Vincenzo, 28, 127, 150
Bellwood, Bessie, 56
Benedict, Julius, 158, 159, 164, 222
Benson, E.F., 89, 155
Berliner, Emile, 106
Berlioz, Hector, 12, 128, 129, 131, 133, 221
Bernhardt, Sarah, 157
Bishop, Henry, 91, 101, 135, 159, 161–3
Blanchard, E.L., 17, 22, 64, 66
Blessington, Countess of, 84
Blockley, John, 91
Boieldieu, F., 28, 201
Bonheur, Rosa, 30
Boosey, William, 221
Booth, William, 48, 51
Boucicault, Dion, 162, 225
Bradley, Reverend E., 22
Brahms, J., 145
BRASS BANDS, 96, 174, 197–203
BROADSIDES, 211–14
Brookes, Shirley, 64

Brookfield, Charles, 44
Brookfield, Mrs., 87
Brough, William, 64
Browning, Robert, 83
Brunn, George le, 57
Bulteel, Mary, 75–6
Bunn, Alfred, 158, 159, 162–4
BURLESQUE, 30, 60–8
Burnand, F.C., 24, 64–8
Burney, Charles, 149, 150
Bushfield, W.F., 227
Byron, Henry, 64, 68

Carlyle, Jane, 141
Carpenter, J. E., 91, 93
Caryll, Ivan, 72
Catnach, James, 211–13
Cavendish, Lady Frederick, 81, 96, 165, 181, 183
Cerito, Francesca, 168–70, 173
Champion, Harry, 57
Chappell, Thomas, 219–21
Chappell, William, 206, 207
Cherry, J. W., 94
Cherubini, M., 131
Chevalier, Albert, 56, 57
Child, Francis, 211
Chopin, F., 83–5, 87, 96
Clifton, Harry, 56, 58
Coborn, Charles, 225
Collcutt, T. E., 157
COMIC OPERA, 69–71
Costa, Michael, 142, 169, 170, 222
Coward, Henry, 118
Cowell, Sam, 21, 22, 37
Cowen, F., 153
Cox, J. E., 130
Curwen, John, 115–20, 221

D'Albert, Charles, 13
DANCING, 14, 176–88, 216–18
DANCING SALOONS, 184–5
Darling, Miss, 94
Deacon, James, 225
Debain, A., 97, 108
Dickens, Charles, 18, 65, 112, 115, 124, 189, 219, 220
Dilke, Charles, 55, 56
Distin, 199
Donizetti, G., 28, 128
D'Oyly Carte, Richard, 157, 221

237

Duncombe, 81
Dvorak, A., 87, 144
Dykes, John, 87
Eaton, Mrs. Glover, 80
Eccles, J. H., 93
Edinburgh, Duke of, 156
Edison, T., 106
Edwardes, George, 44, 72
Egville, M. de, 183
Elgar, Edward, 145, 147
Elssler, Fanny, 167–71, 174
Elssler, Thérèse, 167–9
Ely, Lady, 75, 76
Erard, P., 74, 129
Evans, W. C., 16–19, 21, 22

Fahrbach, 174
Falmouth, Earl of, 84
Favre, Antoine, 98
Fétis, François, 129, 130
Fleury, Louise, 172
FOLK SONG, 14, 15, 19, 205–16
Fox, Harry, 226
Frere, 185
Frith, W., 30

Ganne, 174
Gautier, T., 169
Gay, John, 64
Gilbert, Fred, 59
Gilbert, W. S., 15, 60, 62, 66, 69, 70, 72,
   104, 156, 157, 221, 227
Gladstone, Mary, 80, 96, 139
Gladstone, W. E., 48
Glover, Sarah, 116
Glover, Stephen, 93
Godfrey, Charles, 56, 57
Goldschmitt, Otto, 152
Goschen, George, 35
Gounod, Charles, 33, 141, 144, 174, 221
Grahn, Lucille, 170
Green, Paddy, 19, 21, 22
Grey, Lady de, 141, 154, 155
Grisi, Carlotta, 169, 170
Grisi, Guilia, 149–152
Grossmith, George, 178
Groves, Charles, 129, 143, 162, 171
Guest, Lady Charlotte, 152
Gye, M., 222

Halevy, Jacques, 131
Hall, Owen, 72
Hallé, Charles, 79, 80
Hamilton, Lord Ernest, 150

Hamilton, Kate, 185
Handel, G. F., 126, 130, 138–43, 145, 224
Hardman, William, 53, 54
Hardy, Thomas, 217
Harrison, Clifford, 83
Harrold, 17
Haskell, Arnold, 172
Hatton, John, 83
Haweis, H. R., 119, 139, 154
Hawkins, John, 74
Haydn, Joseph, 101, 130, 131, 145
Haydon, B. R., 30
Haynau, Julius, 50
Heine, H., 170
Hérold, Louis, 15, 201
Herschel, John, 199
Hibble, Charles, 225
Hickson, W. E., 111
Hill, Lady Arthur, 91
Hill, Jenny, 55
Hiller, Ferdinand, 146
Hogarth, George, 123, 124
Hollingshead, John, 68, 69
Hugo, Victor, 170
Hullah, John, 112–20, 125, 145, 146, 162,
   221
Humphrey, Edward, 187
Hunt, Beatrice, 87
Hunter, Harry, 57

Jerrold, Douglas, 18
Jewsbury, Geraldine, 141
Joachim, Joseph, 80, 96
Joel, Herr van, 22
Jones, Sidney, 72, 178
Jullien, Louis, 123, 126–31, 133, 135, 137,
   159, 201, 228

Kay, Dr., 113
Keene, Charles, 62
Kidson, Frank, 206, 207
Kilvert, Francis, 216
Kingsley, Charles, 119, 139
Koenig, 126, 201
Kossuth, Louis, 50

Landseer, Edwin, 18
Lane, S., 28
Lanner, Joseph, 174
Lawrence, Katie, 56, 57
Leather, Ella, 214
Lecocq, Alexandre, 178
Leech, John, 62, 196
Leigh, Percival, 24

Lemon, Mark, 70
Leno, Dan, 56, 57
Leotard, 57
Leybourne, George, 44, 46, 48, 53, 57, 59,
    226
Liddell A. G. C., 183
Lind, Jenny, 13, 83, 149–52, 163
Lindsay, Lady, 91
Liszt, Franz, 76, 85, 122
Lloyd, Arthur, 43, 44, 47, 54
Lloyd, Marie, 56, 57, 208, 224
Lochmann, P., 102
Loder, Edward, 157
Loftus, Cissie, 224
Londesborough, Lord, 225
Longfellow, Henry, 91
Lumley, Benjamin, 151, 170
Lynn, Vera, 47
Lyttleton, Lucy, 81, 96, 165, 181, 183

Macdermott, G. H., 37, 44, 46–8, 54, 55,
    224, 227
Macfarren, George, 157
Mackay, Charles, 222
Mackenzie, Alexander, 143, 144
Maclise, Daniel, 30
Macready, William, 158
McWilliams, 225
Mainzer, Joseph, 113
Manns, August, 133
Mario, 149–55
Marzials, Theo, 212
Matthews, Henry, 55
Mayhew, Henry, 18, 212
Maynard, Ambrose, 226
MECHANICAL MUSIC, 13, 14, 98–110,
    191–4
Melba, Nellie, 154, 155
Mellon, Alfred, 133
Mendelssohn, Felix, 12, 78, 80, 101, 130,
    131, 138, 139, 143, 145, 147, 160, 223,
    224
Messager, 157
Meyerbeer, Giacomo, 128
Milburn, Herbert, 199
MILITARY BANDS, 174, 203, 204
Monckton, Lionel, 72
Montez, Lola, 167
Moody, D. L. R., 48
Morley, Henry, 63
Morton, Charles, 30, 33, 35, 173
Moschelles, Ignaz, 80
Mozart, W. A., 130, 138, 205
Musard, P., 124–6

MUSICAL BOXES, 98–106
MUSICAL COMEDY, 72–3
MUSIC HALL, 11, 14, 26–59, 160, 174,
    175, 224–7
MUSIC IN THE HOME, 12, 14, 74–97,
    99–106, 181

Napoleon III, 35
Newman, Ernest, 205
Nicholson, Renton, 25

Offenbach, J., 70, 173
OPERA, 12, 15, 28, 33, 128–30, 149–64,
    221, 222
ORATORIO, 12, 119, 121, 138–47,
    222–4
OUTDOOR MUSIC, 13, 189–204

Palmerston, Lord, 50
Parry, Hubert, 47, 144, 174, 208
Pascoe, S., 93
Patti, Adelina, 152, 163
Payne, John, 159
Pearsall, R. L., 207
Pettitt, Arthur, 46
PIANO, 13, 14, 74–9, 83–5, 88, 96, 97,
    107–10, 219, 223
Planché, J. R., 30, 61, 62, 68
Pleyel, I., 74
Potter, Cipriani, 154
Pratt, William, 209
Preece, Richard, 30
Prinseps, Val, 80
PROMENADE CONCERTS, 12, 15, 123–
    37, 201, 219

Rachel, Mme, 51
Reeves, Sims, 128, 162, 222
Reszké, Jean de, 154
Rhodes, William, 25
Roberts, Charles, 226
Robson, Frederic, 63, 64
Rogers, E. W., 59
Rosa, Carl, 152, 153, 155
Ross, W. G., 24
Rossetti, D. G., 80
Rossini, G., 28, 131, 150, 165
Rouse, Bravo, 27, 28
Rubens, Paul, 72
Ruskin, John, 11
Russell, Henry, 47, 94

Sacre, Mme, 178
Saint-Saëns, C., 141

Sala, G. A., 18, 64–6
Salisbury, Marchioness of, 181
Sankey, I. D., 48, 104
Santley, Charles, 145, 146
Sartoris, Mrs., 84
Sax, A., 129
Saxe-Coburg, Duke of, 130
Schubert, F., 138, 174, 205
Schumann, Clara, 76, 78, 79
Schumann, Robert, 135
Scott, Clement, 64
Shaftesbury, Earl of, 195, 196
Sharp, Cecil, 205–07, 210
Sharpe, J. W., 21, 22, 47
Shaw, G. B., 143–5, 154
Shaw, Norman, 157
Sherrington, Louise, 56
Sidney, Henry, 19, 21, 58
Sims, 16, 17
Sinclair, George, 227
Sloman, Charles, 19, 47, 58
Smith, Laura, 214
SONG AND SUPPER ROOMS, 16–25
Sousa, John Philip, 104
Spencer, Herbert, 121, 139
Spohr, Louis, 80, 139
Stainer, John, 120
Stanford, C. V., 143, 144
Stephan, Mme Guy, 172
Sterndale Bennett, W., 143, 164
Strange, Frederick, 35
Strauss, Johann, 124, 173
Such, Henry, 213
Sullivan, Arthur, 15, 60, 66, 69, 70, 72,
    89, 104, 156, 157, 174, 178, 221, 227
Sutherland, Duchess of, 84

Tabrar, Joseph, 59
Taglioni, Marie, 13, 164–75
Tenniel, 183

Tennyson, Alfred, 71, 91
Thackeray, W. M., 18, 22, 24, 167
THEATRICAL AGENCIES, 13, 226, 227
Thomas, A., 15, 174
TONIC SOL-FA, 12, 13, 111–22, 221

Vance, Alfred, 44, 46, 53, 225
Vaughan, Kate, 174, 175
Verdi, G., 119, 131, 143
Vestris, Eliza, 60, 61, 161
Victoria, Queen, 12, 75, 76, 96, 127, 145,
    163, 165, 177, 179, 183
Victoria, Vesta, 58

Wagner, Richard, 12, 70, 122, 130, 131,
    133, 149, 153, 154, 156, 202
Waldteufel, Emil, 174
Wales, Prince, of, 12, 42
Wallace, William, 158, 163, 164
Wallerstein, F., 64
Ward, Lord, 165
Ward, Mrs. E. M., 151
Ware, George, 226
Watts, G. F., 80
Weatherley, Fred, 91
Weber, C. M. von, 80, 151, 164
Wellington, Duke of, 178
Wey, Francis, 187
Whistler, J. M., 43
Wilde, Oscar, 43, 87, 161
Wilhem, 113
Wood, Henry J., 135
Woolner, Thomas, 80
Wright, Rosina, 64
Wylde, Henry, 137, 221, 222

Yates, Edmund, 18
Yates, G., 177

Zazel, 50